Firefighter 1 and 2

Exam Study Guide

Mark D. Harris M.D. Editor

Edited and Annotated by Mark D. Harris
Cover design by Nancy Harris

2020

MD Harris Institute Publishing

eBook ISBN 978-1-7343617-4-2
Print ISBN 978-1-7343617-5-9

Preface

Since getting my Fire Safety merit badge in Boy Scouts as a young teen, I have been interested in being a volunteer firefighter. A physician by trade and a retired Army officer, I appreciated the service, the comradery, and the challenge of fighting fires, rescuing lost people, and the hundreds of other things that firefighters do. In September of 2018 joined the Volunteer Fire Department in Beaver, West Virginia. I began Firefighter 1 class that same month.

I am used to reading textbooks and taking tests, but I had never done anything close to firefighting before, except for a short stint as an Emergency Medical Technician 30 years ago. I didn't know a spanner wrench from a minuteman lay, and the 1200-page textbook was a little daunting even for a seasoned test-taker like myself, so I buckled down and started studying.

My firefighter 1 class had 26 students, and almost all of them had some prior firefighting experience. I had none. The classes began with lectures, within my comfort zone. The practical parts were a little less comfortable. Donning the bunker gear vaguely resembled putting on Mission Oriented Protective Posture (MOPP) gear in the Army. The Self-Contained Breathing Apparatus (SCBA) was not wholly dissimilar from the scuba gear that I used in diving.

Some parts of our practical training were totally different than what I had experienced before. I had the pleasure of getting thrown around by a 2 ½ inch charged hose line. Forcible entry seemed almost illegal. Crawling in full bunker gear with SCBA through a box strewn with ropes designed to entangle you suggested that fire is not the only threat that we face. Cutting a hole in a roof with a chainsaw was unusual. But nothing was like crawling into the firebox. It was pitch dark except for the orange-red glow of the flames, at almost 200 degrees (which felt like 400). I have been in combat but had never experienced an environment like fire.

My instructors were patient with me…very patient. Dozens of times I asked myself why I was such a fish out of water, but I pressed on. I passed the written and the practical tests and became a full-fledged volunteer firefighter in November of 2018. Since then I have learned aircraft firefighting, ropes and rescue, dive, ice rescue, fire investigation, firefighter 2, and emergency vehicle operation.

Our team is busy, answering over 1,000 calls per year. I enjoy going on as many as I can, but being a firefighter is as much about community service, and maintaining and cleaning the apparatuses and the stations, as it is about fighting fires. It is mopping, sweeping, cleaning hoses, filling tanks, preincident surveys, and debriefing colleagues with PTSD. It is fund raising, Christmas parties, picnics, fire safety education, and riding on engines in parades.

Of our 26 students, many did not pass. Almost everyone did well on the practical skills, but many stumbled on the written exam. Some couldn't read well, and others could read but were terrified of tests. Many of these men were better firefighters than I am. Many dreamed of making fire a career. To help people like this, I have taken the list of practice questions that we received from our department, about 1200, and gone through the textbook and other references and recorded the answers. I do not know where they got the questions. I have added my notes from several firefighter classes in the past two years. My firefighting career is young, and there is more that I do not know than that I do know. Nonetheless, I have published this study guide to help people who want to be firefighters.

This study guide is dedicated to the outstanding men and women of the Volunteer Fire Department in Beaver, WV. Their skills, patience, friendship, and dedication to duty have served our community and blessed me in ways that they will never know.

Introduction

Citizens call firefighters for almost everything, from high rise structure fires to thousand-acre wildfires to overdoses to motor vehicle accidents to missing person searches to swift water rescues to dive body recoveries. The National Fire Protection Agency summarizes calls that fire departments across America receive every year.[1]

Year	Total	Fires	Medical aid	False alarms	Mutual aid	HAZMAT	Other hazardous conditions	Other
1980	10,819,000	2,988,000	5,045,000	896,500	274,000			1,615,500*
1981	10,594,500	2,893,500	5,019,000	788,000	349,500			1,544,500*
1982	10,548,000	2,538,000	5,258,000	853,500	346,500			1,552,000*
1983	10,933,000	2,326,500	5,660,000	979,500	353,000			1,614,000*
1984	11,070,000	2,343,000	5,735,000	972,000	413,500			1,606,000*
1985	11,888,000	2,371,000	6,467,000	936,500	389,500			1,724,000*
1986	11,890,000	2,271,500	6,437,500	992,500	441,000	171,500	318,000	1,258,000
1987	12,237,500	2,330,000	6,405,000	1,238,500	428,000	193,000	315,000	1,328,000
1988	13,308,000	2,436,500	7,169,500	1,404,500	490,500	204,000	333,000	1,270,000
1989	13,409,500	2,115,000	7,337,000	1,467,000	500,000	207,000	381,500	1,402,000
1990	13,707,500	2,019,000	7,650,000	1,476,000	486,500	210,000	423,000	1,443,000
1991	14,556,500	2,041,500	8,176,000	1,578,500	494,000	221,000	428,500	1,617,000
1992	14,684,500	1,964,500	8,263,000	1,598,000	514,000	220,500	400,000	1,724,500
1993	15,318,500	1,952,500	8,743,500	1,646,500	542,000	245,000	432,500	1,756,500
1994	16,127,000	2,054,500	9,189,000	1,666,000	586,500	250,000	432,500	1,948,500
1995	16,391,500	1,965,500	9,381,000	1,672,500	615,500	254,500	469,500	2,033,000
1996	17,503,000	1,975,000	9,841,500	1,816,500	688,000	285,000	536,500	2,360,500
1997	17,957,500	1,795,000	10,483,000	1,814,500	705,500	271,500	498,500	2,389,500
1998	18,753,000	1,755,500	10,936,000	1,956,000	707,500	301,000	559,000	2,538,000
1999	19,667,000	1,823,000	11,484,000	2,039,000	824,000	297,500	560,000	2,639,500
2000	20,520,000	1,708,000	12,251,000	2,126,500	864,000	319,000	543,500	2,708,000
2001	20,965,500	1,734,500	12,331,000	2,157,500	838,500	381,500	605,000	2,917,500
2002	21,303,500	1,687,500	12,903,000	2,116,000	888,500	361,000	603,500	2,744,000
2003	22,406,000	1,584,500	13,631,500	2,189,500	987,000	349,500	660,500	3,003,500

---

[1] Fire department calls, https://www.nfpa.org/News-and-Research/Data-research-and-tools/Emergency-Responders/Fire-department-calls#:~:text=Fire%20department%20calls%20%20Year%20%20,%20%202%2C889%2C000%20%2021%20more%20rows%20.

2004	22,616,500	1,550,500	14,100,000	2,106,000	984,000	354,000	671,000	2,851,000
2005	23,251,500	1,602,000	14,375,000	2,134,000	1,091,000	375,000	667,000	3,009,000
2006	24,470,000	1,642,500	15,062,500	2,119,500	1,159,500	388,500	659,000	3,438,500
2007	25,334,500	1,557,500	15,784,000	2,208,500	1,109,500	395,500	686,500	3,593,000
2008	25,252,500	1,451,500	15,767,500	2,241,500	1,214,500	394,500	697,500	3,485,500
2009	26,534,500	1,348,500	17,104,000	2,177,000	1,296,000	397,000	625,500	3,586,500
2010	28,205,000	1,331,500	18,522,000	2,187,000	1,189,500	402,000	660,000	3,913,000
2011	30,098,000	1,389,500	19,803,000	2,383,000	1,252,000	379,000	720,000	4,171,500
2012	31,854,000	1,375,000	21,705,500	2,238,000	1,326,500	360,000	694,000	4,155,000
2013	31,644,500	1,240,000	21,372,000	2,343,000	1,298,000	366,500	678,000	4,347,000
2014	31,644,500	1,298,000	20,178,000	2,488,000	1,446,500	405,000	615,000	5,214,000
2015	33,635,500	1,345,500	21,500,000	2,566,500	1,492,500	442,000	643,000	5,646,000
2016	35,320,000	1,342,000	22,750,500	2,622,000	1,515,000	425,000	684,500	5,981,000
2017	34,683,500	1,319,500	22,341,000	2,547,000	1,353,000	423,500	693,000	6,006,000
2018	36,746,500	1,318,500	23,551,500	2,889,000	1,512,500	426,000	706,500	6,342,500

The total number of calls have more than tripled since 1980. At the same time, the number of firefighters has stayed about the same, but the number of volunteer firefighters has dropped.[2] The following table details the number of firefighters in the U.S.

Year	Total	Career	Volunteer
1983*	1,111,200	226,600	884,600
1990	1,025,650	253,000	772,650
2000	1,064,150	286,800	777,350
2010	1,103,300	335,150	768,150
2015	1,149,300	345,600	814,850
2016	1,090,100	361,100	729,000
2017	1,056,200	373,600	682,600

Almost 70% of firefighters were volunteers in 2017, down from over 80% in 1983. Volunteer firefighters tend to serve in rural and suburban areas with fewer resources, and do critical, lifesaving work every day. Recruitment, training, and retention are key problems in volunteer firefighting. This study guide should be used alongside reputable textbooks in Fire Services, not replace them. I ask that any readers who find mistakes let me know at MDHarrisInstitute@gmail.com. Most of the answers in this guide are found in FUNDAMENTALS OF FIREFIGHTER SKILLS, THIRD EDITION, JONES AND BARLETT, 2017. We will use the

---

[2] NEW NFPA REPORT FINDS SIGNIFICANT DECLINE IN VOLUNTEER FIREFIGHTER NUMBERS
April 16, 2019, https://www.nvfc.org/new-nfpa-report-finds-significant-decline-in-volunteer-firefighter-numbers/

abbreviation FFS. Other references come from Lange Current Diagnosis and Treatment, Occupational and Environmental Medicine, Fifth Edition, 2014.

Table of Contents

Chapter 1	Orientation and History of the Fire Service	1
Chapter 2	Firefighter Safety	8
Chapter 3	Personal Protective Equipment (PPE) and Self Contained Breathing Apparatus (SCBA)	15
Chapter 4	Fire Service Communication	22
Chapter 5	Incident Command System	33
Chapter 6	Fire Behavior	46
Chapter 7	Building Construction	58
Chapter 8	Portable Fire Extinguishers	71
Chapter 9	Tools and Equipment	84
Chapter 10	Ropes and Knots	94
Chapter 11	Response and Size up	106
Chapter 12	Forcible Entry	121
Chapter 13	Ladders	132
Chapter 14	Search and Rescue	143
Chapter 15	Ventilation	155
Chapter 16	Water Supply	167
Chapter 17	Fire Attack and Foam	185
Chapter 18	Firefighter Survival – not included	198
Chapter 19	Salvage and Overhaul	199
Chapter 20	Rehabilitation	208
Chapter 21	Wildland and Ground Fires	218
Chapter 22	Fire Suppression	230
Chapter 23	Preincident	248
Chapter 24	Fire and Emergency Medical Care	266
Chapter 25	Emergency Medical Care	275
Chapter 26	Vehicle Rescue and Extrication	294
Chapter 27	Assisting Special Rescue Teams	307
Chapter 28	HAZMAT – not included	320
Chapter 29	HAZMAT – not included	320
Chapter 30	HAZMAT – not included	320
Chapter 31	HAZMAT – not included	320
Chapter 32	HAZMAT – not included	320
Chapter 33	HAZMAT – not included	320
Chapter 34	HAZMAT – not included	320
Chapter 35	Terrorism Awareness – not included	320
Chapter 36	Fire Prevention and Public Education	321
Chapter 37	Fire Detection, Protection, and Suppression Systems	322
Chapter 38	Fire Cause Determination	326

Chapter 1
The Orientation and History of the Fire Service

1. Where was the first fire insurance company formed in America?
    A. Chicago, Illinois
    B. Charleston, South Carolina
    C. New York, New York
    D. Boston, Massachusetts

Answer – B
Reference – FFS, p 17

2. Which term can be defined as the set of guidelines that a department establishes for its fire fighters?
    A. Discipline
    B. Training
    C. Unity of command
    D. Span of control

Answer – A
Reference - FFS, p 12

3. Which style of leadership does the fire department use?
    A. Top centralized
    B. Distributed
    C. Decentralized
    D. Paramilitary

Answer - D
Reference - FFS, p 12

4. Who is responsible for coordinating the activities of several fire companies in a defined geographic area such as a district?
    A. Section chief
    B. Captain
    C. Battalion chief
    D. Assistant chief

Answer - C
Reference - FFS, p 11

Chapter 1

5. The earliest known fire department was in:
   A. The Ottoman Empire
   B. Greece
   C. Ancient Rome
   D. Germany

Answer - C
Reference - FFS, p 13

6. A fire fighter who is trained and certified in chemical identification, leak control, and decontamination is a(n)
   A. Fire Fighter 1
   B. Spill management technician
   C. Hazardous materials technician
   D. Materials technical specialist

Answer - C
Reference - FFS, p 7

7. Which development led to the widespread use of the mechanized pumping apparatus?
   A. Wagon-mounted steam engines
   B. Jacketed hose
   C. Internal combustion engines
   D. Private insurance companies

Answer - C
Reference - FFS, p 16

8. What does the Golden Rule mean when applied to the fire service?
   A. Working as a team is essential to success
   B. Treat everyone else as if they were a member of your family
   C. Stay humble and teachable, and be willing to teach others
   D. Honor the job by working hard and doing your best

Answer - B
Reference - FFS, p 4

9. Which national organization writes codes and standards for fire protection?
    A. United States Fire Administration (USFA)
    B. Occupational Safety and Health Administration (OSHA)
    C. National Fire Protection Association (NFPA)
    D. Federal Emergency Management Agency (FEMA)

Answer - C
Reference - FFS, p 14

10. A fire fighter with specialized training for aircraft and airport-related incidents is a(n)
    A. Aircraft rescue fire fighter
    B. Hazardous material technician
    C. Technical rescue technician
    D. Aviation operations specialist

Answer - A
Reference - FFS, p 7

11. The goal of _____ is to ensure that all members of an agency perform a given task in a uniform way.
    A. Standard operating procedures
    B. The manual of operations
    C. Tactical objectives
    D. Policies

Answer – A
Reference - FFS, p 8

12. Approximately what percent of fire fighters in the United States are volunteers?
    A. 34
    B. 46
    C. 55
    D. 73

Answer - D
Reference - FFS, p 18

Chapter 1

13. Which type of company is responsible for securing a water source, deploying handlines, and putting water on the fire?
   A. Engine
   B. Initial attack
   C. Pumper
   D. Truck

Answer - A
Reference - FFS, p 8

14. Which are the two levels of NFPA fire fighter certification?
   A. A and B
   B. Basic and Advanced
   C. Junior and Senior
   D. One (I) and two (II)

Answer - D
Reference - FFS, p 5

15. In the fire service, the bugle has become a symbol of
   A. Fraternity
   B. Courage
   C. Service
   D. Authority

Answer - D
Reference - FFS, p 17

16. NFPA standards are:
   A. Administrative law
   B. Consensus documents
   C. Regulatory law
   D. Model codes

Answer - B
Reference - FFS, p 14

17. Three out of four career fire fighters work in jurisdictions with a population of _____ or more.
    A. 25,000
    B. 50,000
    C. 75,000
    D. 100,000

Answer - A
Reference - FFS, p 18

18. Training and performance qualifications for firefighters are specified in which NFPA standard?
    A. 472
    B. 1001
    C. 1021
    D. 1500

Answer - B
Reference - FFS, p 5

19. A fire fighter will most typically report directly to a person of which rank?
    A. Battalion chief
    B. Section chief
    C. Lieutenant
    D. Unit leader

Answer - C
Reference - FFS, p 11

20. Which position specializes in reviewing plans for fire detection and suppression systems for functionality and code compliance?
    A. Fire systems specialist
    B. Fire prevention officer
    C. Fire marshal
    D. Fire protection engineer

Answer - D
Reference - FFS, p 7

Chapter 1

21. What does the "S" stand for in "SOP"?
    A. Specific
    B. Special
    C. Standard
    D. Sequential

Answer – C, Standard Operating Procedures
Reference - FFS, p 8

22. Which of the following are developed to provide definitive guidelines for present and future actions?
    A. Regulations
    B. Policies
    C. Standard operating procedures
    D. After-action reports

Answer – B
Reference - FFS, p 8

23. In a typical fire department rank structure, an assistant chief reports directly to the:
    A. Battalion chief
    B. Section chief
    C. Command staff
    D. Chief of the department

Answer – D
Reference - FFS, p 11

24. Which type of company specializes in incidents involving spilled or leaking hazardous chemicals?
    A. Engine
    B. Truck
    C. Hazardous material
    D. Salvage

Answer – C
Reference - FFS, p 10

25. Which basic management principle says that each fire fighter should answer to only one supervisor?
    A. Span of control
    B. Organizational accountability
    C. Unity of command
    D. Division of labor

Answer – C
Reference - FFS, p 12

26. In the fire service, division of labor is necessary to:
    A. Establish chain of command.
    B. Reduce span of control
    C. Prevent duplication of effort.
    D. Assign discipline.

Answer - C
Reference - FFS, p 12

Notes on Fire Organization

Leadership
1. Chief of the Department - Assistant Chief - Battalion Chief - Captain - Lieutenant - Firefighter
2. Assistant Chief (Operations) - Battalion Chief - Captains (Station 1, Station 2, Station 3, etc.)
3. Assistant Chief (Fire Marshall) - Fire Protection Engineer, Fire Inspector(s)

Company types and duties
1. Engine - secure water source, deploy handlines, conduct search and rescue operations, extinguish fire
2. Truck - forcible entry, ventilation, roof operations, search and rescue, deployment of ground ladders
3. Rescue - rescuing victims from fires, confined spaces, trenches, swift water, and high angle
4. Wildland/brush
5. HAZMAT – toxic industrial chemicals (TICs) and toxic industrial materials (TIMs), other toxins
6. Emergency medical services – Emergency Medical Technicians (Basic Life Support - BLS) and Paramedic (Advanced Life Support - ALS)

Chapter 2
Firefighter Safety

1. At least one member of every interior firefighting team should be equipped with a
    A. Portable radio
    B. Thermal imager
    C. Spare SCBA cylinder
    D. Guide rope

Answer - A
Reference - FFS, p 35

2. What is the purpose of a personnel accountability system?
    A. Ensure completion of tasks delegated to fire fighters
    B. Prevent freelancing
    C. Track personnel and assignments on the emergency scene
    D. Brief newly arriving crews on the situation status

Answer - C
Reference - FFS, p 35

3. When is it acceptable to drive a fire apparatus over a downed power line?
    A. If the wire is motionless and silent
    B. Only if it can be done in such a way that no two tires touch the downed line simultaneously
    C. In an emergency situation where there is no alternative approach
    D. Never

Answer - D
Reference - FFS, p 36

4. The majority of fire fighter injuries are:
    A. Soft-tissue injuries
    B. Strains and sprains
    C. Burns
    D. Inhalation injuries

Answer - B
Reference - FFS, p 27

5. Which of the following is an essential element of safe emergency operations?
   A. Initiative
   B. Sacrifice
   C. Teamwork
   D. Integrity

Answer - C
Reference - FFS, p 35

6. The majority of fire fighter deaths are caused by:
   A. Heart attack or stroke
   B. Trauma
   C. Burns
   D. Asphyxiation

Answer - A
Reference - FFS, p 26

7. If you observe an unsafe practice during training, what should you do?
   A. Stay focused on your own assignment
   B. Alert the members in closest proximity to the hazard
   C. Take immediate action to reduce the hazard
   D. Bring it to the attention of the instructor or designated safety officer

Answer - D
Reference - FFS, p 30

8. Which part of the body should be used for a heavy lift?
   A. The waist
   B. The legs
   C. The abdomen
   D. The shoulder girdle

Answer - B
Reference - FFS, p 36

Chapter 2

9. Who should accompany a fire fighter sent to the rehabilitation area?
   A. No one; the affected fire fighter should go to rehab alone
   B. One member of his or her crew
   C. The entire crew
   D. An EMT

Answer - C
Reference - FFS, p 36

10. What is the minimum number of fire fighters required to make up a firefighting team?
    A. 1
    B. 2
    C. 3
    D. 4

Answer - B
Reference - FFS, p 35

11. Which statement best summarizes the types of incidents for which the incident command system (ICS) be should be implemented?
    A. All emergency incidents
    B. Incidents involving more than a single company
    C. Incidents where the incident commander's span of control is exceeded
    D. Incidents exceeding a single operational period

Answer - A
Reference - FFS, p 27

12. Who has the authority to directly and immediately stop any activity on the fire ground that he or she judges to be unsafe?
    A. All personnel
    B. Company officer
    C. Division/group supervisors
    D. Safety officer

Answer - D
Reference - FFS, p 28

13. How soon after a traumatic call should a critical incident stress debriefing (CISD) be held?
    A. As soon as possible
    B. Within 24 hours
    C. Within 72 hours
    D. Within a week

Answer - A
Reference - FFS, p 37

14. It is estimated that one vehicle accident involving an emergency vehicle occurs for every how many emergency responses:
    A. 100
    B. 1000
    C. 5000
    D. 10,000

Answer - B
Reference - FFS, p 27

15. Which statement about downed electrical wires is correct?
    A. Turnout boots and thick rubber gloves will afford you sufficient protection.
    B. A downed power line may be safely pinned down under the tire of the apparatus.
    C. Fire fighters should operate under the assumption that all downed utility lines are energized.
    D. Fire fighters should use tools with wood or fiberglass handles to manipulate downed lines.

Answer - C
Reference - FFS, p 36

16. When is freelancing acceptable during emergency operations?
    A. Prior to the establishment of an incident command structure
    B. In response to sudden changes in circumstances or conditions
    C. Whenever such action will result in a favorable outcome
    D. Never

Answer - D
Reference - FFS, p 28

Chapter 2

17. What is a common sign or symptom of heat stroke?
    A. Hot, dry skin
    B. Cramping
    C. Profuse sweating
    D. Bradycardia

Answer - A
Reference - FFS, p 37

18. A primary goal of investigating each fire fighter accident or injury is to:
    A. Establish patterns and trends
    B. Assess civil liability exposure
    C. Determine whether misfeasance occurred
    D. Determine how such an incident can be avoided in the future

Answer – D
Reference - FFS, p 26

19. What is the term for acting without a superior's orders or outside of department SOPs?
    A. Independent action
    B. Initiative
    C. Decentralized authority
    D. Freelancing

Answer - D
Reference - FFS, p 28

20. What is the relationship between habits developed in training and performance on the fire ground?
    A. In the stress of emergency operations, habits are overridden by instincts
    B. Habits formed in training necessarily become abbreviated and rushed on the fire ground
    C. Habits developed in training will continue on the fire ground
    D. Fire-ground performance is not significantly altered through habituation

Answer - C
Reference - FFS, p 28

Firefighter Safety

21. If one team member must exit a hazard area for any reason, what should the rest of the team do?
    A. Continue working on their assignment
    B. Assign a buddy to accompany the member out of the hazard area
    C. Exit as the entire team together
    D. Defer to the team leader, who should decide based on the circumstances

Answer - C
Reference - FFS, p 35

22. In the United States, what is the ratio of fire fighter deaths that occurs during emergency operations to number that occur during nonemergency activities?
    A. Nearly five times
    B. About twice
    C. About half
    D. About equal to

Answer - D
Reference - FFS, p 26

23. Who is responsible for determining when removal of SCBA is permissible after a fire has been extinguished?
    A. Each individual is responsible for this decision
    B. The company officer
    C. The incident commander
    D. The safety officer

Answer - D
Reference - FFS, p 28

24. When responding to domestic disputes or other scenes involving violence, fire fighters should:
    A. Attempt to mediate the dispute
    B. Wait for law enforcement to declare the scene safe
    C. Call for a critical incident stress debriefing team
    D. Remove the involved individuals to separate rooms

Answer - B
Reference - FFS, p 38

25. Approximately ____ fire fighters are killed in the line of duty each year in the United States.
    A. 10
    B. 100
    C. 1000
    D. 10,000

Answer – B
Reference - FFS, p 26

Notes on Firefighter Safety

Guidelines for safe emergency vehicle response
1. Drive defensively
2. Follow appropriate policies regarding posted speed limits. Driving faster rarely gets firefighters to the scene more quickly.
3. Stay four seconds behind the vehicle in front of you.
4. Keep an open space next to you (open lane or safe shoulder) so that you can swerve to avoid an accident if the vehicle in front of you stops suddenly.
5. Assume other drivers will not hear your siren or see your lights.
6. Use the shortest and least congested route to the scene.
7. Visually clear all direction of an intersection before going into it.
8. Drive with the flow of traffic.
9. Avoid all bystanders and pedestrians.

Safety at emergency incidents
1. Stay with your team (at least two people per team) and do not work alone.
2. Each team is accountable for its members
3. Apparatus leader is accountable for every member on that apparatus
4. Safety officer is accountable for each firefighter at the incident (through the apparatus leaders while maintaining span of control.
5. Incident commander is accountable for everyone at the incident (through the safety officer)
6. Use tools and equipment safely
7. Beware gas, electric, and other fuel or power sources
8. Rehabilitation - separate area for doffing gear, resting, rehydrating

Chapter 3
Personal Protective Equipment (PPE) and Self-Contained Breathing Apparatus (SCBA)

1. Which fire gas is a product of burning plastic?
   A. Acrolein
   B. Hydrogen cyanide
   C. Carbon dioxide
   D. Hydrogen sulfide

Answer - B
Reference - FFS, p 55

2. What is the first step in cleaning self-contained breathing apparatus (SCBA)?
   A. Rinse the entire unit with clean water from a hose
   B. Use compressed air to blow loose contamination off the unit
   C. Remove the cylinder from the harness
   D. Cover the regulator in a plastic bag

Answer - A
Reference - FFS, p 81

3. The thick, quilted layer of a turnout coat is the _____?
   A. Vapor barrier
   B. Liner
   C. Thermal barrier
   D. Absorbent liner

Answer - C
Reference - FFS, p 46

4. Pressure readings on an SCBA cylinder gauge and the regulator or remote pressure gauge should not differ by more than psi.
   A. 50 psi (350 kPa)
   B. 100 psi (700 kPa)
   C. 200 psi (1400 kPa)
   D. 250 psi (1700 kPa)

Answer - B
Reference - FFS, p 64

Chapter 3

5. Which statement about the care and use of PPE is correct?
    A. Damp turnout coats provide an extra degree of thermal protection.
    B. In hot weather, resist the temptation to remove your turnout coat when at the rehabilitation station.
    C. Special cleaning solutions are available for home laundering of turnout coats.
    D. Accumulated dirt or contamination reduces the protective quality of turnout coats.

Answer - D
Reference - FFS, p 51

6. Which gas is most commonly produced by residential or commercial fires?
    A. Anhydrous ammonia
    B. Nitrous oxide
    C. Hydrogen sulfide
    D. Hydrogen cyanide

Answer - D
Reference - FFS, p 55

7. Which component of structural turnout coats is critical for protecting the body from steam burns?
    A. Moisture barrier
    B. Thermal barrier
    C. Outer shell
    D. Insulation

Answer - A
Reference - FFS, p 46

8. NFPA standards require an SCBA low-air alarm to sound when cylinder pressure drops to what percent of capacity?
    A. 10
    B. 15
    C. 20
    D. 25

Answer - D
Reference - FFS, p 60

Personal Protective Equipment (PPE) and Self-Contained Breathing Apparatus (SCBA)

9. Which NFPA standard deals with protective ensembles for structural and proximity firefighting?
   A. 1472
   B. 1500
   C. 1981
   D. 1971

Answer - D
Reference - FFS, p 46

10. Which fire gas kills by replacing oxygen in the blood?
    A. Sulfur dioxide
    B. Hydrogen cyanide
    C. Carbon monoxide
    D. Phosgene

Answer - C
Reference - FFS, p 55

11. Which NFPA standard deals with open-circuit self-contained breathing apparatus?
    A. 1622
    B. 1801
    C. 1981
    D. 1990

Answer - C
Reference - FFS, p 46

12. The primary hazard of this chemical is that it can displace oxygen from the atmosphere:
    A. Carbon monoxide
    B. Hydrogen cyanide
    C. Carbon dioxide
    D. Chlorine

Answer - C
Reference - FFS, p 55

13. How often should SCBA face pieces be fit-tested?
    A. Monthly
    B. Every 3 months
    C. Every 6 months
    D. Every 12 months

Answer - D
Reference - FFS, p 62

14. Which NFPA standard deals with protective clothing and equipment for wildland firefighting?
    A. 1072
    B. 1214
    C. 1977
    D. 1982

Answer - C
Reference - FFS, p 46

15. What is a flame-resistant material used in PPE?
    A. Durex
    B. PBI
    C. Treated cotton duck
    D. Thermax

Answer - B
Reference - FFS, p 46

16. Turnout coats and trousers have a protective system that consists of layers:
    A. 2
    B. 3
    C. 4
    D. 5

Answer - B
Reference - FFS, p 46

Personal Protective Equipment (PPE) and Self-Contained Breathing Apparatus (SCBA)

17. What is the function of an EOSTI?
    A. Emit an audible alarm when the wearer becomes motionless
    B. Broadcast a mayday signal
    C. Emit an audible alarm in the presence of certain gases
    D. Warn an SCBA wearer of low cylinder pressure

Answer - D
Reference - FFS, p 60

18. What is a commonly used technique for conserving SCBA air?
    A. Skip breathing
    B. Breath counting
    C. Pursed-lip breathing
    D. Inhale by mouth, exhale by nose

Answer - A
Reference - FFS, p 62

19. A structural firefighting PPE ensemble includes which specific piece of equipment?
    A. Portable radio
    B. Self-contained breathing apparatus (SCBA)
    C. Thermal imager
    D. Safety harness

Answer - B
Reference - FFS, p 48

20. What is the primary function of the purge valve on an SCBA?
    A. Switch between pressure and pressure-demand modes
    B. Supply air in the event of a regulator malfunction
    C. De-fog the face piece interior
    D. Bleed off residual pressure after the cylinder valve has been closed

Answer - B
Reference - FFS, p 60

Chapter 3

21. What is the primary function of the moisture barrier in structural firefighting PPE?
    A. Keep liquids and vapors from reaching the skin
    B. Protect the body from high temperatures
    C. Promote evaporation of perspiration
    D. Prevent exposure to pathogens

Answer - A
Reference - FFS, p 46

22. Which item is an optional component of the structural firefighting ensemble?
    A. Hearing protection
    B. Personal alert safety system
    C. Protective hood
    D. Eye protection

Answer – A. However, given the loud environment generated by most structure fires, as well as loud equipment such as chain saws, ear plugs should be used consistently.
Reference - FFS, p 49

23. Fire fighters should be able to don personal protective clothing within how many seconds.
    A. 45
    B. 60
    C. 75
    D. 90

Answer - B
Reference - FFS, p 51

24. Which part of the structural firefighting PPE ensemble is designed to protect the neck and ears?
    A. The protective hood
    B. The coat collar
    C. The bib
    D. The SCBA mask

Answer - A
Reference - FFS, p 46

25. What is the realistic duration of an SCBA air supply compared to the rated duration?
    A. About the same
    B. Somewhat longer
    C. Somewhat shorter
    D. Much shorter

Answer – D
Reference - FFS, p 58

26. Which is an acceptable method of cleaning protective gear?
    A. Wash it outside and leave it in the sun to dry
    B. Take it home to clean it in the household washer
    C. Send it to an approved cleaning facility
    D. Take to a commercial laundromat to clean it

Answer – C
Reference - FFS, p 51

Notes on PPE and SCBA

Protection provided by bunker gear
1. Thermal
2. Repels water
3. Impact
4. Cuts and abrasions
5. Padding against injury
6. Respiratory

Gear
1. Helmet (with face shield)
2. Protective hood
3. Turnout coat
4. Bunker pants
5. Boots
6. Gloves
7. Respiratory protection
8. Personal alert safety system

Chapter 3

9. Other - goggles, hearing protection, drag rescue device, reflective safety vest forr highway incidents

Chapter 4
Fire Service Communication

1. Which critical piece of information is required by the telecommunicator to initiate a dispatch?
    A. Nature of the situation
    B. Reporting party identity
    C. Callback number
    D. Severity of the situation

Answer - A
Reference - FFS, p 97

2. What type of phone is designed for use by hearing-impaired persons?
    A. Display
    B. Text
    C. Digital
    D. Video

Answer - B
Reference - FFS, p 97

3. Radio frequencies are designated in units of:
    A. Megahertz
    B. Hertz
    C. Gigahertz
    D. Terahertz

Answer - A
Reference - FFS, p 105

4. The NFPA standard requires that a communications center be equipped with:
    A. HEPA-grade air filtration system
    B. Backup systems for all the critical equipment
    C. A reception area with a staffed watch desk
    D. A private water supply

Answer - B
Reference - FFS, p 93

Chapter 4

5. What happens if a CAD system detects that an invalid address is being entered?
   A. It sends a full first alarm assignment to each possible location
   B. It prompts the telecommunicator to ask the caller for additional information
   C. It offers a best estimate of the correct location
   D. It sends a single unit to the nearest valid location

Answer – B. CAD is Computer Aided Dispatch.
Reference - FFS, p 95

6. Which agency licenses a fire department to operate a radio system?
   A. Federal Communications Commission
   B. The state office of emergency services
   C. Federal Office of Communications
   D. Federal Emergency Management Agency

Answer - A
Reference - FFS, p 104

7. What is the third step in the five-step process of receiving and dispatching an emergency call?
   A. Caller instruction
   B. Unit notification
   C. Unit selection
   D. Classification and prioritization

Answer - D
Reference - FFS, p 96

8. How does the Canadian emergency reporting system differ from the 911 system used in the United States?
   A. Canadian callers must dial seven-digit numbers to report an emergency
   B. Emergency reporting numbers in Canada vary between provinces and territories
   C. Canadian callers must dial "0" to report an emergency
   D. The U.S. and Canadian systems are essentially the same

Answer - D
Reference - FFS, p 95

9. What does the term "mayday" mean?
    A. Everyone must withdraw from the hazard area
    B. A fire fighter is in trouble and needs assistance
    C. Hold all radio traffic
    D. Deploy the rapid intervention crew (RIC)

Answer - B
Reference - FFS, p 109

10. What is the function of the Push to Talk (PTT) button on a two-way radio?
    A. Adjust the sensitivity of signal reception
    B. Enable duplex transmission
    C. Cause the radio to transmit
    D. Transmit a distress signal

Answer - C
Reference - FFS, p 107

11. Which item is a primary factor in determining which units to send to an incident?
    A. The reporting party's recommendation
    B. The time lapse between call receipt and dispatch
    C. The incident location
    D. The reporting party's plausibility

Answer - C
Reference - FFS, p 96

12. What is the term for an urgent message that takes priority over all other communications?
    A. Mayday
    B. Code 30
    C. Emergency traffic
    D. Priority message

Answer - C
Reference - FFS, p 109

Chapter 4

13. What does the "A" stand for in "CAD"?
    A. Aided
    B. Automatic
    C. Auxiliary
    D. Ancillary

Answer – A. "Computer Aided Dispatch" is a common meaning for the acronym.
Reference - FFS, p 94

14. What is the term for a radio signal that alerts personnel to pull back to a safe location?
    A. Withdrawal order
    B. Mayday
    C. Evacuation signal
    D. Emergency traffic

Answer - C
Reference - FFS, p 109

15. What is the correct term for the small two-way radios carried by individual fire fighters?
    A. Mobile radios
    B. Walkie-talkies
    C. Portable radios
    D. Pocket radios

Answer - C
Reference - FFS, p 103

16. What should a call-taker do if a call comes in about an issue the fire department does not handle?
    A. Transfer, direct, or refer the caller to the appropriate agency
    B. Send the call to the back of the queue and take it when there is no priority traffic
    C. Politely inform the caller that the fire department does not provide assistance for his or her issue
    D. Advise the caller to call back on the nonemergency line

Answer - A
Reference - FFS, p 100

Fire Service Communication

17. How has the widespread use of cellular phones affected the automatic location identification (ALI) feature of enhanced 911 systems?
    A. ALI does not function for wireless calls
    B. ALI is not needed
    C. ALI may be unable to provide a specific location
    D. The location database is updated automatically

Answer – C
Reference - FFS, p 99

18. What is the correct term for a radio system permanently mounted in a building?
    A. Base station
    B. Transmitter
    C. Land radio system
    D. Repeater system

Answer - A
Reference - FFS, p 104

19. What does the "A" stand for in "PSAP"?
    A. Alerting
    B. Activating
    C. Auxiliary
    D. Answering

Answer – D, Public Safety Answering Point
Reference - FFS, p 96

20. What is the function of an automatic vehicle locator system?
    A. Determine the location of mobile phone callers
    B. Prioritize resources based upon location
    C. Track apparatus location via GPS
    D. Display fire department vehicle location on an electronic map

Answer - C
Reference - FFS, p 103

Chapter 4

21. What does the "D" stand for in "ADA"?
    A. Dangerous
    B. Disabilities
    C. Distressed
    D. Directional

Answer – B. The "Americans with Disabilities Act (ADA)" was enacted to protect the rights of the disabled.
Reference - FFS, p 97

22. What does the "N" stand for in "ANI"?
    A. Number
    B. Network
    C. Normal
    D. Name

Answer – A. Automatic Number Identification.
Reference - FFS, p 98

23. What is the term for a phone line that connects two predetermined points?
    A. Dedicated circuit
    B. Private line
    C. Local circuit
    D. Direct line

Answer – D. The President's "red phone" to Moscow is a legendary example.
Reference - FFS, p 97

24. Telecommunicators should use what type of listening?
    A. Critical
    B. Active
    C. Interrogatory
    D. Interpretive

Answer – B. Emergency operators have a critical role in getting the correct information quickly and relaying that information to responders well. Operating center personnel deal with hysterical, angry, confused, and otherwise difficult people daily.
Reference - FFS, p 99

Fire Service Communication

25. Which statement about telecommunication center voice recorders is correct?
    A. The recordings are useful for review of the telecommunication center's performance.
    B. The recordings are not discoverable for use in litigation.
    C. Nondisclosure laws require destruction of recordings of routine traffic after 72 hours.
    D. The units record only when manually activated by the telecommunicator.

Answer – A. These recordings are vital legal documents as well.
Reference - FFS, p 95

26. What does the second "D" stand for in "TDD"?
    A. Deaf
    B. Dispatch
    C. Dedicated
    D. Dialer

Answer – A. Telecommunications Device for the Deaf (TDD)
Reference - FFS, p 97

27. What is the term for a two-way radio that is permanently mounted in a vehicle?
    A. Mobile radio
    B. Portable radio
    C. Hi-band radio
    D. Repeater

Answer - A
Reference - FFS, p 103

28. What does the "P" stand for in "GPS"?
    A. Positioning
    B. Proactive
    C. Personnel
    D. Preventive

Answer – A. Global Positioning System.
Reference - FFS, p 94

Chapter 4

29. What is the second step in the five-step process of receiving and dispatching emergency calls?
    A. Classification/prioritization
    B. Location validation
    C. Confirmation
    D. Caller interrogation

Answer - B
Reference - FFS, p 96

30. What is the term for a radio that transmits and receives on different frequencies?
    A. Repeater
    B. Cross-band
    C. Duplex
    D. Binary

Answer - C
Reference - FFS, p 105

31. Approximately what percentage of the United States and Canada has access to a 911 system?
    A. 60
    B. 70
    C. 80
    D. 90

Answer - D
Reference - FFS, p 95

32. A caller is connected directly to a telecommunicator through which device?
    A. Local alarm
    B. Fire alarm box
    C. Central alarm station
    D. Call box

Answer - D
Reference - FFS, p 98

33. Which statement about a wireless phone calling 911 is correct?
    A. Callers may report emergencies without knowing the location.
    B. The calls are automatically prioritized to the rear of the queue.
    C. Enhanced 911 system features eliminate the problem of locating the caller.
    D. The call is routed to a national center, resulting in considerable delay in their receipt by the local telecommunication center.

Answer - A
Reference - FFS, p 97

34. What is the usual response when a caller disconnects before full information can be gathered and the dispatcher cannot reconnect by calling the caller back?
    A. Log the incident and wait for the caller to call back
    B. Send a full complement of responders, including police, EMS, and fire
    C. Dispatch a police unit to check on the caller
    D. Send a single engine to assess the situation

Answer - C
Reference - FFS, p 97

35. What are TDD and TTY?
    A. Location finders in enhanced 911 systems
    B. Routers that direct wireless calls to the appropriate dispatch center
    C. Communication devices for hearing-impaired persons
    D. Voice-activated applications for smart phones that place a 911 call

Answer – C. TTY is "Text Telephone."
Reference - FFS, p 97

36. Fire departments that operate radio equipment must hold radio licenses from the:
    A. National Emergency Broadcasting
    B. Federal Central Communications
    C. Nation Radio Communications
    D. Federal Communications Commission

Answer – D
Reference - FFS, p 104-105

Chapter 4

37. All records and reports generated by the fire department are:
    A. Exempt from legal challenges
    B. Legal documents and must be completed thoroughly
    C. Private and protected under the Freedom of Information Act
    D. Notations and, therefore, do not require accurate narrative information

Answer – B
Reference - FFS, p 110

Notes on Fire Service Communication

Communications Center Equipment
    1. Dedicated 911 telephones
    2. Public telephones
    3. Direct line phones to other agencies
    4. Equipment to receive alarms from public or private fire alarm systems
    5. Computers and/or hard copy maps to locate addresses and dispatch units
    6. Equipment for alerting and dispatching units
    7. Two-way radio system
    8. Recording devices to record phone calls.
    9. Backup electrical generator
    10. Records management system

Five steps in processing emergency calls
    1. Receive call
    2. Validate location
    3. Classification and prioritization
    4. Unit selection
    5. Dispatch

Radios
    1. These options depend on each department's radio system and each county or state protocols
    2. Wear radio in radio pocket of bunker gear, not outside.
    3. Orange button goes to pager mode on county fire. Listener will only hear tones for his department. On any other channel, the orange button is MAYDAY!
    4. County - all law enforcement, EMS, and fire in the county can hear
    5. Fire ground 1 - direct back and forth, push button and talk, fire operations, use it when you arrive on scene

6. Fire ground 2 - direct back and forth, push button to talk, tanker shuttle and other fire operations. Can still hear county on fireground 2.
7. Tactical 1 - General
8. Tactical 2 - General
9. Tactical 3 - General
10. Tactical 4 - General
11. Event 1 - Search and rescue
12. Event 2 - General
13. Private - Limited to one department
14. All radio communications are accessible to people with scanners.

Report (completed after each incident)
1. Where and when the incident occurred
2. Who was involved?
3. What happened
4. How the fire started
5. Extent of damage
6. Injuries or fatalities (civilian and firefighter - both injuries must be reported to State fire marshal and NFPA)
7. Reports are admissible in a court of law. Incomplete or inadequate reports may be used to prove that the fire department was negligent.

Sources of information
1. Property owner and/or occupant - get name, insurance, and phone number
2. Bystanders or eyewitnesses
3. Obtain serial numbers and model numbers of key equipment (washers, dryers, stoves, ovens, washing machines, other electrical equipment).

Coding procedures
1. Incident type (three-digit code)
2. Actions taken (two-digit code)
3. Property use
4. Written guides and/or computer programs provide codes and explanations of codes used in fire reports.

Chapter 5
Incident Command System

1. What is the ICS term for an assembly of two to five single resources gathered to accomplish a specific task?
   A. Strike team
   B. Group
   C. Task force
   D. Division

Answer - C
Reference - FFS, p 127

2. The command staff reports directly to the:
   A. Chief fire official
   B. Command staff director
   C. Operations section chief
   D. Incident commander

Answer - D
Reference - FFS, p 123

3. What is the title for the individual in charge of a company?
   A. Resource director
   B. Squad leader
   C. Company officer
   D. Sector manager

Answer - C
Reference - FFS, p 126

4. What is the ICS title for the person in charge of a task force?
   A. Leader
   B. Director
   C. Officer
   D. Supervisor

Answer - A
Reference - FFS, p 128

Incident Command System

5. Within the ICS, what is the maximum number of people that one person should normally supervise?
   A. 3
   B. 5
   C. 7
   D. 9

Answer - B
Reference - FFS, p 121

6. What is the ICS title for the person in charge of a branch?
   A. Chief
   B. Director
   C. Manager
   D. Supervisor

Answer - B
Reference - FFS, p 127

7. The first-arriving officer at the scene of a serious incident should _____ command.
   A. Establish
   B. Pass
   C. Transfer
   D. Defer

Answer - A
Reference - FFS, p 123

8. The leader of a group has rank equal to that of the leader of a _____.
   A. Division
   B. Branch
   C. Section
   D. Strike team/task force

Answer - A
Reference - FFS, p 126

Chapter 5

9. Which statement best summarizes the type of incident for which ICS is applicable?
   A. Incidents involving unified command
   B. Incidents crossing jurisdiction borders
   C. Incidents exceeding more than one operational period
   D. Any type of incident

Answer - D
Reference - FFS, p 121

10. As more companies are deployed at an incident, why must the incident management structure expand?
    A. To establish personnel accountability
    B. To maintain span of control
    C. To maintain unity of command
    D. To establish the modular organization

Answer - B
Reference - FFS, p 121

11. Which organization developed the first standard incident command system?
    A. NFPA
    B. FEMA
    C. USFA
    D. FIRESCOPE

Answer – D
Reference - FFS, p 119

12. Under which circumstances does the first-arriving officer become command?
    A. Upon arrival of a second officer
    B. When multiple units will be needed to manage the incident
    C. When necessary to maintain span of control
    D. On every incident

Answer - D
Reference - FFS, p 123

Incident Command System

13. What would be the ICS designation for each floor in a high-rise building?
    A. Sector
    B. Section
    C. Division
    D. Group

Answer - C
Reference - FFS, p 128

14. Who serves as the command's point of contact for representatives from outside agencies?
    A. The planning director
    B. The agency representative
    C. The liaison officer
    D. The staging chief

Answer - C
Reference - FFS, p 124

15. What is the ICS term for a group of fire fighters with an assigned leader who are working without an apparatus?
    A. Crew
    B. Group
    C. Team
    D. Unit

Answer - A
Reference - FFS, p 126

16. The ICS title of director is applied to the supervisor of a _____.
    A. Section
    B. Branch
    C. Division
    D. Company

Answer - B
Reference - FFS, p 127

17. Collectively, the section chiefs are known as the _____.
    A. general staff
    B. unified command
    C. tactical group
    D. command staff

Answer - A
Reference - FFS, p 124

18. Which position is part of the command staff?
    A. Safety
    B. Finance/administration
    C. Spokesperson
    D. Planning

Answer - A
Reference - FFS, p 124

19. Which of the following is a location near the incident scene where resources are held, ready to be assigned if needed?
    A. Check-in area
    B. Incident base
    C. Staging area
    D. Camp

Answer - C
Reference - FFS, p 122

20. Which ICS section is responsible for taking direct action to control the incident?
    A. Division
    B. Operations
    C. Tactics
    D. Command

Answer - B
Reference - FFS, p 125

Incident Command System

21. Which statement best describes the concept of unified command?
    A. Each subordinate is accountable to only one supervisor.
    B. All members of the command staff agree to the same set of objectives, tactics, and strategy for the incident.
    C. The chain of command is clearly defined and strictly adhered to.
    D. Representatives from different agencies share command authority.

Answer - D
Reference - FFS, p 123

22. When is command terminated?
    A. When the IC declares "All clear"
    B. When the incident is declared under control
    C. When the IC releases the command and general staff
    D. When the last company leaves the scene

Answer - D
Reference - FFS, p 123

23. In general, the ideal span of control within the ICS is ___ to one.
    A. Three
    B. Four
    C. Five
    D. Seven

Answer - C
Reference - FFS, p 121

24. An exposure on the left side of the fire building would be designated as exposure
    A. Side A
    B. Side B
    C. Side C
    D. Side D

Answer - B
Reference - FFS, p 127

25. Under which condition might command be transferred from a high-ranking officer to an officer with lower rank?
    A. After the third benchmark
    B. If the incident is escalating
    C. During the later stages of the incident
    D. There are no conditions when this is appropriate

Answer - C
Reference - FFS, p 134

26. Which method of communication for sharing transfer-of-command information is most effective?
    A. Face to face
    B. Radio report
    C. Cell phone
    D. Written report with diagrams

Answer - A
Reference - FFS, p 134

27. In which decade did efforts begin to establish a standardized incident command system?
    A. 1950s
    B. 1960s
    C. 1970s
    D. 1980s

Answer - C
Reference - FFS, p 118

28. Which principle requires each person to have only one direct supervisor?
    A. Management by objectives
    B. Unity of command
    C. Span of control
    D. Chain of command

Answer - B
Reference - FFS, p 121

29. The National Incident Management System (NIMS) was developed in response to a(n):
    A. Presidential directive
    B. Federal administrative law
    C. National consensus standard
    D. Act of Congress

Answer - A
Reference - FFS, p 118

30. What is the ICS term for resources working within the same geographical area?
    A. Branch
    B. Group
    C. Division
    D. Unit

Answer - C
Reference - FFS, p 126

31. What is a basic ICS concept that applies to every incident?
    A. Every fire fighter always reports to a single supervisor
    B. Command is passed to the second-in unit upon its arrival
    C. Command is always transferred to a ranking officer
    D. The operations section chief is activated on every incident

Answer - A
Reference - FFS, p 121

32. In the ICS structure, who is the one person ultimately responsible for managing an incident?
    A. The executive officer
    B. The planning chief
    C. The incident commander
    D. The operations section chief

Answer - C
Reference - FFS, p 123

Chapter 5

33. Which ICS section is responsible for developing the Incident Action Plan (IAP)?
    A. Command
    B. Operations
    C. Tactical
    D. Planning

Answer - D
Reference - FFS, p 125

34. Which term describes representatives from several different agencies working together to manage a multijurisdictional incident in a coordinated manner?
    A. Group command
    B. Area command
    C. Operational control
    D. Unified command

Answer - D
Reference - FFS, p 120

35. What is the ICS term for companies or crews working on the same task or function?
    A. Division
    B. Group
    C. Unit
    D. Branch

Answer - B
Reference - FFS, p 126

36. Which characteristic is an advantage of unified command?
    A. Delegates decision making to a single incident commander
    B. Maintains and reinforces the span of control
    C. Eliminates the need for unity of command
    D. Reduced conflict and duplication of effort

Answer - D
Reference - FFS, p 120

Incident Command System

37. Which phrase best summarizes the smallest operations for which an ICS should be established?
    A. Incidents involving multiple agencies
    B. Incidents involving multiple units
    C. Operations in IDLH atmospheres
    D. Everyday operations

Answer - D
Reference - FFS, p 121

38. Which of the following is a key characteristic of the incident command system?
    A. Common terminology
    B. Professional financial accounting
    C. Decentralized command authority
    D. Sharing of human resources

Answer - A
Reference - FFS, p 122

39. What is the ICS term for an assembly of five units of the same type with an assigned leader?
    A. Strike team
    B. Unit
    C. Section
    D. Task force

Answer - A
Reference - FFS, p 128

40. Who would usually be assigned the role of operations section chief?
    A. The senior officer
    B. A chief officer with a strong background in operations
    C. The ranking officer
    D. The first-arriving officer

Answer - B
Reference - FFS, p 125

Chapter 5

41. Which of the following is an ICS single resource?
    A. Unit
    B. Company officer
    C. Strike team
    D. Engine company

Answer - D
Reference - FFS, p 126

42. Which of the following is a key characteristic of the incident command system?
    A. Resource conservation
    B. Consolidated incident action plans
    C. Preincident planning
    D. Reciprocal aid agreements

Answer - B
Reference - FFS, p 122

43. Which description best summarizes the "modular organization" of the ICS?
    A. The ability to expand the span of control along with the incident
    B. Clearly defined and limited areas of responsibility and authority
    C. Seamless incorporation of personnel from several different agencies
    D. A management structure that can expand to match the needs of the situation

Answer - D
Reference - FFS, p 121

44. If there is no officer on the first-arriving unit, who assumes initial command?
    A. The first officer to arrive
    B. The driver/operator
    C. The senior fire fighter
    D. Whomever the nearest responding chief officer designates over the radio

Answer - C
Reference - FFS, p 131

45. Who is responsible for determining the strategic incident objectives?
    A. Command staff
    B. Planning officer
    C. Incident commander
    D. Operations section chief

Answer - C
Reference - FFS, p 120

46. Under normal conditions, only a/an _____ may order multiple alarms or additional resources for large scale incidents.

    A. Incident commander
    B. Safety operations officer
    C. Planning officer
    D. Logistics officer

Answer - A
Reference - FFS, p 131

47. The two most common ways the incident commander orders firefighters to evacuate a structure are to broadcast a radio message and:
    A. Sound an audible warning
    B. Page all firefighters to respond
    C. Implement an accountability system
    D. Contact dispatch to activate PASS device

Answer - A
Reference - FFS, p

48. In the Incident Management System, who is the one person ultimately responsible for managing an incident?
    A. The Operations Chief
    B. A Chief Officer
    C. The Planning Chief
    D. The Incident Commander

Answer - D
Reference - FFS, p 123

Chapter 5

49. What would be the incident command designation for the 7th floor of a high-rise?
    A. Seventh floor
    B. Level 7
    C. Division 7
    D. Sector 7

Answer - C
Reference - FFS, p 128

Notes on Incident Command System

Organizational Breakdown
1. Single resource - a vehicle and its assigned personnel
2. Crew - group of firefighters without apparatus
3. Division - geographical area distribution of resources (sides of buildings - ABCD, floors in a building - 1, 2, 3, 4, etc.)
4. Group - functional distribution of resources. A group must have an apparatus. Otherwise, it is a crew.
5. Branch - oversees several divisions or groups
6. Task force - up to five single resources of any type (i.e. two engines, one ladder, and two rescue trucks)
7. Strike team - up to five units of the same type (i.e. five engines, often all brush fire vehicles)

Chapter 6
Fire Behavior

1. What is the second phase of fire?
   A. Growth
   B. Flameover
   C. Fully developed
   D. Incipient

Answer - A
Reference - FFS, p 151

2. What is the percentage of oxygen normally found in air?
   A. 14.7 percent
   B. 18 percent
   C. 19.5 percent
   D. 21 percent

Answer – D. Environmental air (outdoors) is roughly 21% oxygen, 78% nitrogen, and other trace gases. Indoor air may be slightly less if the ventilation (number of air exchanges) is adequate. Carbon dioxide can displace oxygen and present a dangerous environment. Expired air is roughly 16% oxygen.
Reference - FFS, p 143

3. A gas with a vapor density of ____ will rise in air.
   A. 0.1
   B. 1.0
   C. 10
   D. 100

Answer – A. Any gas with a density of less than one will rise in air, such as helium or hydrogen. A gas with a density of 1.0 will neither rise nor fall. Gases with densities of greater than one, such as chlorine gas will fall in air. That is one reason that the trenches in World War 1 became so toxic.
Reference - FFS, p 157

Chapter 6

4. Which form of heat transfer travels in all directions?
   A. Convection
   B. Thermal radiation
   C. Conduction
   D. Direct contact

Answer - B
Reference - FFS, p 148

5. What is the smallest unit of matter?

   A. A molecule
   B. A visible particle
   C. An element
   D. An atom

Answer – D. Subatomic particles such as protons, neutrons, and electrons are not considered.
Reference - FFS, p 144

6. Which form of energy causes spontaneous heating of a pile of linseed oil-soaked rags?
   A. Organic
   B. Hypergolic
   C. Exothermic
   D. Chemical

Answer - D
Reference - FFS, p 143

7. Flammable liquid fires are considered Class:
   A. A
   B. B
   C. C
   D. D

Answer - B
Reference - FFS, p 148

Fire Behavior

8. What is the term for the lowest temperature at which a liquid produces enough vapor to sustain a continuous fire?
   A. Vaporization temperature
   B. Flash point
   C. Flame point
   D. Ignition temperature

Answer - C
Reference - FFS, p 157

9. What is the relationship between resistance and heat as electricity flows through a wire?
   A. There is no relationship between the two
   B. As resistance increases, heat increases
   C. As resistance decreases, heat increases
   D. As resistance increases, heat decreases

Answer - B
Reference - FFS, p 143

10. What is the term for high-volume, high-velocity, turbulent, ultra-dense black smoke?
    A. Turbulent fire
    B. Black fire
    C. Endothermic fire
    D. Laminar fire

Answer - B
Reference - FFS, p 159

11. Friction is a form of energy.
    A. Radiant
    B. Molecular
    C. Mechanical
    D. Kinetic

Answer - C
Reference - FFS, p 143

Chapter 6

12. Which of the following is a side of the fire triangle?
    A. Catalyst
    B. Heat
    C. Chemical chain reaction
    D. Ignition source

Answer – B. The fire triangle includes heat, oxygen, and fuel.
Reference - FFS, p 144

13. Which form of heat transfer consists of kinetic energy moving from one particle to another?
    A. Induction
    B. Reduction
    C. Conduction
    D. Convection

Answer - C
Reference - FFS, p 146

14. Flashover occurs during which phase of fire?
    A. Growth
    B. Incipient
    C. Fully developed
    D. Ignition

Answer – A
Reference - FFS, p 152

15. What is a term for rapid oxidation that produces heat and light?
    A. Combustion
    B. Catalyzation
    C. Vaporization
    D. Pyrolysis

   Answer - A
Reference - FFS, p 145

Fire Behavior

16. What is the vapor density of air?
   A. 0.0
   B. 1.0
   C. 14.7
   D. 29.9

Answer - B
Reference - FFS, p 157

17. What is the lowest temperature at which a fuel—air mixture will ignite spontaneously called?
   A. Fire point
   B. Ignition temperature
   C. Flash point
   D. Specific heat

Answer - B
Reference - FFS, p 143

18. The sudden introduction of air into an oxygen-depleted, superheated space may result in

   A. Improved visibility
   B. Ghosting
   C. Backdraft
   D. Black fire

Answer - C
Reference - FFS, p 153

19. Which geometric figure is used to represent the four elements required for a self-sustaining fire?
   A. Pyramid
   B. Square
   C. Polygon
   D. Tetrahedron

Answer - D
Reference - FFS, p 144

Chapter 6

20. What is the term for temperature in a room reaching the point where all the combustible contents of the room ignite?
    A. Autoignition
    B. Flashover
    C. Backdraft
    D. Rollover

Answer - B
Reference - FFS, p 152

21. Which of the following is a component of a BLEVE?
    A. A pressurized flammable liquid vessel
    B. A "closed box" structure
    C. A flammable gas leak
    D. Contact with an energized electrical circuit

Answer - A
Reference - FFS, p 157

22. What is the term for the lowest temperature at which a liquid produces enough flammable vapor to burn momentarily?
    A. Fire point
    B. Ignition temperature
    C. Flammable range
    D. Flash point

Answer - D
Reference - FFS, p 156

23. Smoke that is produced by ordinary household materials when they are first heated has which sort of appearance?
    A. Mustard yellow and lazy
    B. Slow moving and white
    C. Brown and fast moving
    D. Black and thick

Answer - B
Reference - FFS, p 159

Fire Behavior

24. A chemical reaction that produces heat is:
    A. Exothermic
    B. Thermodynamic
    C. Isothermic
    D. Endothermic

Answer - A
Reference - FFS, p 143

25. What is the term for the spontaneous ignition of hot gases at the upper level of a room?
    A. Ghosting
    B. Flashover
    C. Flameover
    D. Mushrooming

Answer - C
Reference - FFS, p 152

26. Which situation is indicated when you open a door and the smoke exits through the top half of the door and clean air enters through the bottom half?
    A. Disturbance of thermal layering
    B. An under-ventilated fire
    C. The fire is on the same level as the door
    D. Nonsurvivable conditions for occupants

Answer – C. Thermal layering occurs because hot gases rise, and cooler gases sink in air. The hot gases are at higher pressure, causing the upper layer to push out on top. The resulting partial vacuum sucks cool air in below. The fire is probably on the same level as the door.
Reference - FFS, p 160

27. The movement of heated gases in a fire is an example of which form of heat transfer?
    A. Circulation
    B. Radiation
    C. Conduction
    D. Convection

Answer - D
Reference - FFS, p 147

Chapter 6

28. Heat transfer in the form of invisible waves is called:
    A. Conduction
    B. Radiation
    C. Convection
    D. Emission

Answer - B
Reference - FFS, p 147

29. When water is converted to steam, it occupies space.
    A. Mmuch more
    B. Somewhat more
    C. About the same
    D. Somewhat less

Answer - A
Reference - FFS, p 143

30. What is a danger to consider when attacking a Class C fire?
    A. Electrical injury
    B. Flashover
    C. Permeation of PPE
    D. Backdraft

Answer – A. If possible, always turn off the electricity to burning electrical equipment. This will change the fire into a Class A or B fire, which can be fought with Class A or B equipment.
Reference - FFS, p 149

31. Upward spread of fire within a structure is primarily caused by which form of heat transfer?
    A. Circulation
    B. Radiation
    C. Conduction
    D. Convection

Answer - D
Reference - FFS, p 147

Fire Behavior

32. A Class C fire involves _____.
    A. A flammable liquid or gas
    B. Energized electrical equipment
    C. Cooking material
    D. A combustible metal

Answer – B. Cutting off the power to the building de-energizes the electrical equipment.
Reference - FFS, p 149

33. Which sign is an indication of possible backdraft conditions?
    A. Turbulent, pressurized smoke
    B. Vigorous flame productions
    C. Windows broken out
    D. Good interior visibility

Answer - A
Reference - FFS, p 153

34. An endothermic reaction is one that _____.
    A. Requires a catalyst
    B. Absorbs heat
    C. Occurs in the absence of oxygen
    D. Releases energy

Answer – B. Campfires are exothermic reactions. Reactions with freon and other cooling agents are endothermic. That is why refrigerators and freezers work.
Reference - FFS, p 143

35. The majority of fires are extinguished by which method?
    A. Cooling the fuel
    B. Excluding oxygen
    C. Suppressing vapor emission
    D. Inhibiting the chemical chain reaction

Answer - A
Reference - FFS, p 148

Chapter 6

36. What is the method of choice for extinguishing most Class B fires?
    A. Excluding the oxygen
    B. Cooling the fuel
    C. Interrupting the chemical chain reaction
    D. Dispersing the vapors

Answer - A
Reference - FFS, p 149

37. Which state must a fuel be in for combustion to take place?
    A. Solid
    B. Liquid
    C. Vapor
    D. Solid, liquid, or vapor

Answer – C. Liquid fuels such as gasoline and kerosene do not burn, but the vapor layer just above the fuel burns. Solid fuels such as wood burn with the vapor produced by cellulose via pyrolysis.
Reference - FFS, p 142

38. What is another term for flammability limits?
    A. Explosive limits
    B. Volatility index
    C. Oxidation range
    D. Pyrophoric limits

Answer - A
Reference - FFS, p 157

39. During this phase, fire has consumed either the available fuel or oxygen, and temperature drops.
    A. Isothermic
    B. Overhaul
    C. Incipient
    D. Decay

Answer - D
Reference - FFS, p 154

40. The flash point of gasoline is:
    A. -45°F (-43°C)
    B. -15°F (-26°C)
    C. -0°F (-18°C)
    D. 32°F (0°C)

Answer - A
Reference - FFS, p 157

41. Prior to making entry into a structure fire, firefighters should consider:
    A. Establishing rehab
    B. Reading the smoke conditions and fire behavior
    C. The location of the Incident Safety Officer
    D. The location of staging area

Answer - B
Reference - FFS, p 158

Notes on Fire Behavior

Classes of Fires
1. Class A - ordinary combustibles like wood and paper
2. Class B - liquids like spilled fluids
3. Class C - electrical fires
4. Class D - combustible metals such as sodium, magnesium, titanium
5. Class K - combustible cooking oils and fats in kitchens

Solid fuel fires
1. Wood burns more slowly and with less heat release than petrochemical-based solids.
2. Moisture cools a fire environment, and wood with higher water content is more difficult to burn than wood with lower water content.
3. Fuel - more fuel results in a hotter burn
4. Surface to mass ratio - the energy required to ignite substances with a high surface to mass ratio is less than the energy required to ignite substances with a low surface to mass ratio. Restated, energy requirement is inversely proportional to the surface to mass ratio. This applies to liquids and gases as well.
5. Orientation - A board placed horizontally will burn more slowly than one placed vertically
6. Continuity - The closer one piece of fuel is to another, the more likely the fire is to spread, and the more quickly it will spread.

Chapter 6

Fire stages
1. Incipient stage - The initial fuel is ignited, and the fire is small. There is little increase in the temperature of the room. Fire is fuel dependent.
2. Growth stage – Fire is often oxygen dependent.
3. Flashover – Highest danger of flashover
4. Fully developed
5. Decay

Modern structural fire environment
1. Characteristics - Large home + open floor plan + large fuel load + void spaces + building materials + smaller lots + new technologies
2. Dangers - Faster fire propagation, shorter time to flashover, rapid changes in fire dynamics, shorter escape time, shorter time to collapse, increased exposure problems, new and unexpected hazards

Smoke reading
1. Attributes - volume, velocity, density, color
2. Black Fire - high density, high velocity, turbulent, ultra-dense black smoke which indicates temperatures around 1000 F and imminent worsening and flashover.

Chapter 7
Building Construction

1. Which type of construction is called ordinary construction?
    A. I
    B. II
    C. III
    D. IV

Answer – C. Fast food restaurants and stores at strip malls typically have this sort of construction.
Reference - FFS, p 176

2. What is Type V construction?
    A. Fire resistive
    B. Wood frame
    C. Ordinary
    D. Lightweight

Answer – B. Homes typically have this kind of construction.
Reference - FFS, p 177

3. What is another term for gypsum board?
    A. Lath
    B. OSB
    C. Drywall
    D. Stucco

Answer - C
Reference - FFS, p 171

4. Which term refers to how a building is used?
    A. Classification
    B. Occupancy
    C. Group
    D. Type

Answer - B
Reference - FFS, p 168

Chapter 7

5. Type II construction is referred to as:
   A. Ordinary
   B. Fire resistive
   C. Fire retardant
   D. Noncombustible

Answer – D. These buildings are built of concrete, steel, and other non-burning materials like Type 1 buildings are. However, they do not have specific fire-resistant properties like Type 1 buildings do.
Reference - FFS, p 175

6. Which construction type is particularly susceptible to extension of fire upward through walls?
   A. Balloon frame
   B. Ordinary
   C. Heavy timber
   D. Platform

Answer – A. Homes built in the US and Europe from 1830s to the 1950s may have this type of construction.
Reference - FFS, p 178

7. Which tool is commonly used to provide a secure work platform for fire fighters working on a pitched roof?
   A. Roof ladder
   B. Halligan
   C. Pike pole
   D. Safety rope

Answer - A
Reference - FFS, p 182

8. Fire-retardant wood is treated with _____.
   A. Aluminum oxide
   B. Mineral salts
   C. Calcium sulfate
   D. Urea

Answer - B
Reference - FFS, p 173

9. Which type of truss has a curved upper member and a straight lower member?
   A. Lightweight
   B. Engineered
   C. Open web
   D. Bowstring

Answer - D
Reference - FFS, p 185

10. Which term is a measure of whether a material will burn?
    A. Conductivity
    B. Combustibility
    C. Pyrolytic index
    D. Specific heat

Answer - B
Reference - FFS, p 169

11. Which type of construction is heavy timber?
    A. II
    B. III
    C. IV
    D. V

Answer – C. Older houses have heavy timber construction.
Reference - FFS, p 176

12. Which term describes how readily heat will flow through a material?
    A. Thermal conductivity
    B. Combustibility
    C. Volatility
    D. Reactivity

Answer - A
Reference - FFS, p 169

Chapter 7

13. The structural components of a Type _____ building will not burn.
    A. II
    B. III
    C. IV
    D. V

Answer - A
Reference - FFS, p 175

14. Which type of wall is used to prevent the spread of fire from one side of the wall to the other?
    A. Curtain
    B. Bearing
    C. Fire
    D. Partition

Answer - C
Reference - FFS, p 169

15. Which is the primary fire hazard of ordinary construction?
    A. Fire extension through concealed spaces
    B. High fire loading
    C. Difficulty in ventilating the structure
    D. Heat-related failure of steel trusses

Answer - A
Reference - FFS, p 176

16. What is the term for plastics that will melt under fire conditions?
    A. Thermoset
    B. Amorphous
    C. Thermoplastic
    D. Pyrolytic

Answer - C
Reference - FFS, p 173

17. What is a bar joist?
    A. Any engineered component with steel load-bearing members
    B. A truss with steel parallel members and wood diagonals
    C. An open-web steel truss
    D. A steel I-beam used to support a floor or roof

Answer - C
Reference - FFS, p 184

18. What is plasterboard commonly used for?
    A. Shear wall
    B. Roof fascia and soffits
    C. Roof sheathing
    D. Interior walls and ceilings

Answer - D
Reference - FFS, p 171

19. What is the most common application for an engineered wood product?
    A. Short load-bearing members
    B. Where high fire-resistance is required
    C. Where extra-long beams are required
    D. Stair treads and risers

Answer - C
Reference - FFS, p 172

20. Which statement about masonry materials is correct?
    A. Masonry materials are susceptible to pyrolysis.
    B. Masonry materials have high thermal conductivity.
    C. Masonry materials expand significantly when heated.
    D. Masonry materials are fire resistive.

Answer - D
Reference - FFS, p 169

21. What is another term for gypsum board?
    A. Chalkboard
    B. Paneling
    C. Cement board
    D. Sheetrock

Answer - D
Reference - FFS, p 171

22. What is Type IV construction?
    A. Wood frame
    B. Masonry on synthetics
    C. Heavy timber
    D. Synthetics

Answer - C
Reference - FFS, p 176

23. What is the term for building components consisting of individual pieces of wood glued together?
    A. Engineered
    B. Lightweight
    C. Modular
    D. Manufactured

Answer - A
Reference - FFS, p 172

24. Which metal is used in building construction primarily as a coating to protect metal parts from rust and corrosion?
    A. Zinc
    B. Copper
    C. Manganese
    D. Gypsum

Answer - A
Reference - FFS, p 170

25. What does steel do when heated?
    A. Contract
    B. Harden
    C. Elongate
    D. Spall

Answer - C
Reference - FFS, p 169

26. What is one of the four key characteristics affecting the behavior of building materials under fire conditions?
    A. Composition
    B. Combustibility
    C. Load
    D. Stability

Answer - B
Reference - FFS, p 169

27. What is the term for the chemical change that occurs to wood when it is heated?
    A. Catagenesis
    B. Pyrolysis
    C. Reduction
    D. Oxidization

Answer - B
Reference - FFS, p 172

28. Which material is commonly used to protect steel and wood structural members from
    A. Gypsum
    B. Fiberglass
    C. Lightweight concrete slurry
    D. Expanded urethane

Answer - A
Reference - FFS, p 171

29. Which construction feature is most commonly found in Type V buildings?
    A. Pre-stressed concrete
    B. Treated lumber
    C. Bar joists
    D. Platform-frame construction

Answer - D
Reference - FFS, p 172

30. Gypsum board that is exposed to fire for a prolonged time will
    A. Spall
    B. Fail
    C. Delaminate
    D. Warp

Answer - B
Reference - FFS, p 171

31. What is a commonly used structural material in a Type I building?
    A. Treated wood
    B. Engineered wood
    C. Protected steel
    D. Oriented-strand board

Answer - C
Reference - FFS, p 174

32. Which statement about structural steel is correct?
    A. Structural steel is strong under both tension and compression.
    B. Temperatures commonly produced in fires exceed structural steel's melting point.
    C. Structural steel maintains its shape when exposed to high temperatures.
    D. Structural steel is susceptible to fatigue.

Answer - A
Reference - FFS, p 170

33. Type III construction is usually limited to a maximum height of _____ stories.
   A. 2
   B. 3
   C. 4
   D. 5

Answer - C
Reference - FFS, p 176

34. In which condition does moisture trapped in concrete become heated, turn into steam, and expand, causing parts of the concrete to break away?
   A. Cavitation
   B. Scaling
   C. Spalling
   D. Stressing

Answer - C
Reference - FFS, p 170

35. Which type of glass is most typically used in fire doors and windows?
   A. Pyrex
   B. Laminated
   C. Wired
   D. Safety

Answer - C
Reference - FFS, p 171

36. Spalling of concrete could lead to early collapse in Type I buildings because:
   A. Reinforcing steel is exposed to the heat of the fire
   B. It could create void spaces
   C. The added weight of broken pieces may cause overload
   D. Loss of moisture in concrete reduces its fire rating

Answer - A
Reference - FFS, p 170

37. Structure members that are of noncombustible materials but may not have fire resistive protection are identified as:
   A. Type I
   B. Type III
   C. Type IV
   D. Type II

Answer - D
Reference - FFS, p 175

38. The usual cause of collapse of a lightweight steel truss is the:
   A. Poor construction methods
   B. Amount of heat generated by the fire in a structure
   C. Cooling effects of water
   D. Impact load of firefighters jumping onto roof

Answer - B
Reference - FFS, p 186

39. A _____ is designed to prevent the spread of fire within a structure or between adjacent structures.
   A. Fire wall
   B. Stop
   C. Partition
   D. Truss

Answer - A
Reference - FFS, p 187

Notes on Fast Food Restaurants

Do not bring a residential mindset into a commerical fire situation

LODD - McDonald's fire - Kim Smith (30), Louis Mayo III (44) killed, 14 Feb 2000, Houston TX, heavy fog, slowed down response.

Specific
   1. Roofs flat, but often hidden behind fake wall on the perimeter
   2. Lots of wiring in ceiling, which can falls through the dropped ceiling and entangle firefighters.

3. Back doors in all stores in all strip malls are the same - metal door with deadbolt in metal frame. This door should be opened and stopped early to allow entry and exit.
4. Dropped ceilings act to slow down fires, keping them from heating the roof supports and causing roof collapse
5. Is this a contents fire or a structural fire.

Ventilation (fire and life)
1. Let hot air escape and cool air in.
2. Bring fire to a certain exit point.
3. Vent for life - cool down environment and direct fire away from victims.
4. Vertical - dangerous to put people on a lightweight truss roof
5. Horizontal - fastest way to ventilate an area.
6. Positive pressure fans - forces air into an area. Fog nozzle (2.5 inch hose) on a hose can force smoke out of an area.

Positive Pressure Attack (fan is tactical part of fire attack) vs. Positive Pressure Ventilation (remove smoke after the fire is knocked down)

1. Exhaust - Opening should be 2-3 times the size of the inlet ventilation point. Fan position should be 4-6 ft back and 15 degree tilt above horizontal. This leaves a 12-16 inch gap at the top of the door to see what is happening inside.
2. Entry - Do not start the fans if the crew is in the structure. Do not use fans if you don't know where the fire is.
3. Execution - Ventilating a ventilation-limited fire will enlarge the fire and may cause flashover. Make sure that the exit area is very large and that everyone knows the plan.

When not to use PPA or PPV:
1. Backdraft conditions
2. Volatile environment
3. Victim at potential exhaust vent
4. Leeward fire attack in high winds (less than 15 mph) - fans will not overcome high winds.

Large CO_2 tanks used to carbonate beverages can leak and produce an oxygen deficient environment.

Known restaurant hazards
1. Greases
2. Plastics
3. Gases

Chapter 7

Notes on Modern Buildings

Severity, Urgency, and Growth (SUG)
1. Severity - How bad is the situation? What is at risk (lives, property, etc.)
2. Urgency - How much time do I have to accomplish this goal?
3. Growth - Will the situation get much worse if I don't act? Will my immediate action effectively impair growth?

Building types
1. Type 1 - Fire resistive - building (steel, concrete, gypsum board) materials are not themselves fuel for the fire. Fire resistance for at least two hours.
2. Type 2 - Noncombustible - fire resistance rating of 1-2 hours, single story warehouse or factory buildings, maximum of two stories
3. Type 3 - Ordinary (Brick and Joist) - typical commercial construction, malls and strip malls. Combination of building materials, some are fuel and some are not.
4. Type 4 - Heavy Timber - through the 1940s. Building materials are fuel for the fire.
5. Type 5 - Wood Frame - most commonly used today, up to four stories in height. Fire prevention is with fire detection devices and automatic sprinklers. Structure is just strong enough to support the expected load and no stronger. Building materials are fuel for the fire.

Construction notes
1. Balloon frame construction - Studs run continuously from basement to roof. Fire can move to all floors more easily.
2. Platform frame construction - first floor is built as a platform and the studs for the exterior walls are erected on top of it. This style prevents fire from spreading from one floor to another through continuous stud spaces.
3. Party wall - load bearing wall used by two different buildings. It is vulnerable to fire spread, especially when penetrated by wiring, plumbing, etc.
4. Fire wall - fire barrier, frequently outside walls, usually extend from the building foundation up to the roof.
5. Fire partitions - interior walls that extend from a floor to the underside of the floor above.
6. Fire enclosures - prevents fire and smoke from moving vertically from floor to floor.
7. Curtain walls - non-weight-bearing exterior walls attached to the building structure. A non-weight bearing wall supports only its own weight.
8. Solid, load-bearing masonry walls at least 6-8 inches thick can support a building up to six stories tall.

Primary tenets of operations

1. Resistance - how can I keep the fire out of an area?
2. Resilience - if the fire gets in, how long before the area fails?
3. Integrity - how will the building stay up with us in or around it?
4. Time - how much time do we have?
5. Compromise - isolated failure
6. Collapse - complete failure

What are the characteristics of the building's collapse if it happens? Modern normal construction buildings (class 5) are much more likely to collapse than older, heavy timbered ones (class 4).

The single biggest factor in fire related failure is not related to construction but related to products of combustion in the building. Books, papers, plastics, and other combustibles are present in higher concentrations in the modern buildings. Therefore, fires have more fuel, burn hotter, and burn faster.

Building factors determining likelihood of building failure
1. Building anatomy (era, components)
2. Building occupancy (type, risk use (commercial, residential), era, components, etc),
3. Building susceptibility to compromise and collapse
4. Fire Dynamics - energy, speed
5. Methods and materials of construction

Compression (system with support redundancies) vs tension (interdependent systems, if one part fails, everything else does too.)

Chapter 8
Portable Fire Extinguishers

1. What residue does a CO2 fire extinguisher leave when discharged?
   A. Carbon
   B. Iron oxide
   C. Mineral salt
   D. None

Answer - D
Reference - FFS, p 207

2. Which extinguishing method is being used when a foam blanket is placed over the surface of a burning liquid?
   A. Cutting off the oxygen supply
   B. Inhibiting the chemical chain reaction
   C. Diluting the fuel
   D. Cooling the fuel

Answer - A
Reference - FFS, p 208

3. All fire extinguishers are classified according to:
   A. the net weight of their contents
   B. their relative extinguishing power
   C. the classes of fire on which they are effective
   D. the type of extinguishing agent used

Answer - C
Reference - FFS, p 202

4. For extinguisher selection and placement, what is an example of a light hazard environment?
   A. Self-storage building
   B. Classroom
   C. Parking garage
   D. Restaurant kitchen

Answer - B
Reference - FFS, p 204

Portable Fire Extinguishers

5. A Class C extinguisher is rated for use on:
   A. Radioactive materials involved in flame
   B. Eenergized electrical equipment
   C. Flammable chemicals
   D. Wood, paper, or cloth

Answer - B
Reference - FFS, p 201

6. What does it mean when a fire extinguisher has a pictograph with a red slash through it?
   A. Use on that class of fire would be ineffective
   B. Use on that class of fire could be hazardous
   C. The fire extinguisher has not been tested for use on that class of fire
   D. The fire extinguisher is rated for use on that class of fire

Answer - B
Reference - FFS, p 203

7. The "P" in the acronym PASS, used in reference to fire extinguisher operation, stands for:
   A. Point
   B. Pick
   C. Pause
   D. Pull

Answer – D. "PASS" is Pull the pin, Aim the nozzle at the base of the fire, Squeeze the handle, and Sweep the fire from side to side.
Reference - FFS, p 218

8. Which statement about the numerical rating of a Class K extinguisher is correct?
   A. There is no numerical rating for a Class K extinguisher.
   B. The numerical rating indicates the relative extinguishing power of the agent.
   C. The numerical rating indicates the relative duration of the agent.
   D. A numerical rating is required for commercial hood systems.

Answer - A
Reference - FFS, p 209

Chapter 8

9. Which class of fire is depicted in the pictograph system by a flame and an electrical plug and socket?
   A. K
   B. B
   C. C
   D. D

Answer - C
Reference - FFS, p 203

10. Which agent is approved for use in a Class K system?
    A. Wet chemical
    B. Aqueous film-forming foam
    C. Carbon dioxide
    D. Dry chemical

Answer - A
Reference - FFS, p 202

11. Which class of fire includes cloth?
    A. A
    B. B
    C. C
    D. D

Answer - A
Reference - FFS, p 200

12. According to NFPA 10, the maximum floor area that can be protected by each extinguisher depends on the _____.
    A. Presence of a built-in suppression system
    B. Occupancy type
    C. Construction class
    D. Occupancy load

Answer - B
Reference - FFS, p 203

Portable Fire Extinguishers

13. What is used to pressurize a stored-pressure water extinguisher?
    A. Compressed air
    B. Nitrogen
    C. Water
    D. Carbon dioxide

Answer - A
Reference - FFS, p 211

14. Which hazard category includes automotive service or repair facilities?
    A. Severe
    B. Moderate
    C. Ordinary
    D. Extra

Answer - D
Reference - FFS, p 205

15. A potential problem with application of a multipurpose dry chemical agent to a Class K fire is:
    A. Neutralization of other agents applied to the fire
    B. Production of toxic gas
    C. Spitting and splattering of fuel
    D. Sudden flare-up of the fire

Answer - A
Reference - FFS, p 214

16. Which extinguishing agent is suitable for use on a Class C fire?
    A. Carbon tetrachloride
    B. Carbon dioxide
    C. Dry powder
    D. Aqueous film-forming foam (AFFF)

Answer - B
Reference - FFS, p 201

17. Which of the following is commonly used as a dry chemical extinguishing agent?
    A. Calcium bicarbonate
    B. Carbon tetrachloride
    C. Potassium hydrate
    D. Ammonium phosphate

Answer - D
Reference - FFS, p 207

18. Which statement about dry chemical agents is correct?
    A. Dry chemical agents are noncorrosive.
    B. Dry chemical agents are compatible with all types of foam.
    C. All dry chemical agents have a multipurpose rating.
    D. Dry chemical agents are not subject to freezing.

Answer - D
Reference - FFS, p 206

19. In general, the maximum reach of a CO_2 extinguisher is _____ feet.
    A. 32
    B. 16
    C. 8
    D. 4

Answer - C
Reference - FFS, p 214

20. When approaching a fire with an extinguisher in hand, you should always have a(n) _____.
    A. Exit route
    B. Backup unit
    C. Light source
    D. Portable radio

Answer - A
Reference - FFS, p 220

Portable Fire Extinguishers

21. A portable fire extinguisher is bested suited for which situation?
    A. Car fire
    B. Room and contents fire
    C. Fire in a wastebasket
    D. Vegetation fire

Answer - C
Reference - FFS, p 199

22. What is the best way to extinguish a Class C fire?
    A. Withdraw to a safe distance and let the fire burn itself out
    B. Shut off the power and treat it as a Class A or B fire
    C. Use a Class C extinguisher
    D. Shut off the fuel flow at a valve

Answer - B
Reference - FFS, p 201

23. Which statement is correct regarding Class D extinguishing agents?
    A. Application methods are similar regardless of the agent and fuel involved.
    B. The specific agent must be matched to the specific fuel.
    C. Most agents are effective on several Class D fuels.
    D. Some agents are also rated for other classes of fire.

Answer - B
Reference - FFS, p 201

24. For an area to qualify for the classification of "light hazard," most of the combustibles present must be:
    A. Extinguishable by a portable fire extinguisher
    B. Arranged so that a fire is unlikely to spread
    C. No more than moderately combustible
    D. Class A only

Answer - B
Reference - FFS, p 204

Chapter 8

25. To qualify as a light hazard for the purpose of extinguisher selection and placement, the majority of materials in the area must _____.
    A. Be fire resistive
    B. Be class A or C combustibles
    C. Have a flash point exceeding 150⁰ F
    D. Be noncombustible

Answer - D
Reference - FFS, p 204

26. What is one disadvantage of CO_2 extinguishers?
    A. Electrical conductivity
    B. Cost
    C. Short discharge range
    D. Corrosive residue

Answer - C
Reference - FFS, p 207

27. For fire extinguisher placement, what is the relationship between occupancy use category and hazard classification?
    A. They are not necessarily related
    B. Occupancy determines hazard
    C. Hazard determines occupancy
    D. They are different terms for the same thing

Answer - A
Reference - FFS, p 204

28. Which class of fire includes flammable and combustible liquids?
    A. A
    B. B
    C. C
    D. D

Answer - B
Reference - FFS, p 200

Portable Fire Extinguishers

29. What is the most commonly used extinguishing agent for Class A fires?
   A. Water
   B. Ammonium phosphate
   C. Dry chemical
   D. Potassium bicarbonate

Answer - A
Reference - FFS, p 200

30. How do multipurpose dry chemical agents prevent rekindling of Class A fuel?
   A. By forming a crust over the fuel
   B. By penetrating the fuel
   C. By attracting and holding moisture
   D. By interrupting the chemical chain reaction

Answer - A
Reference - FFS, p 207

31. Class D agents work primarily by:
   A. Penetrating the fuel
   B. Forming a crust over the fuel
   C. Suppressing vapor production
   D. Inhibiting the chemical chain reaction

Answer - B
Reference - FFS, p 224

32. What is a correct use for a portable fire extinguisher?
   A. Pretreating exposures
   B. Diluting flammable liquids
   C. Situations in which the use of water is not recommended
   D. Overhaul

Answer - C
Reference - FFS, p 199

Chapter 8

33. Requirements for placing and mounting portable fire extinguishers are found in NFPA _____.
    A. 10
    B. 170
    C. 470
    D. 1201

Answer - A
Reference - FFS, p 203

34. Which fire extinguishing agent is best for use on sensitive electronic equipment?
    A. Loaded stream
    B. Carbon dioxide
    C. Aqueous film-forming foam (AFFF)
    D. Ammonium phosphate

Answer - B
Reference - FFS, p 201

35. Which motion best accomplishes the removal of the pin and tamper seal from a portable fire extinguisher?
    A. A strong pull directly outward
    B. Twisting motion
    C. Side-to-side motion
    D. Push, then pull

Answer - B
Reference - FFS, p 210

36. A fire extinguisher's agent is stored within its:
    A. Tank
    B. Horn
    C. Chamber
    D. Cylinder

Answer - D
Reference - FFS, p 210

Portable Fire Extinguishers

37. What is an advantage of portable fire extinguishers over hose lines?
    A. Greater heat absorption
    B. Controllable rates of flow
    C. Longer duration
    D. Faster deployment

Answer - D
Reference - FFS, p 199

38. Which class of fire involves combustible cooking oils and fats?
    A. K
    B. A
    C. B
    D. D

Answer - A
Reference - FFS, p 201

39. Which class of fire is depicted in the pictograph system by a fire in a frying pan?
    A. K
    B. A
    C. B
    D. D

Answer - A
Reference - FFS, p 203

40. For the purpose of extinguisher selection and placement, light hazard environments usually contain a limited amount of combustibles of which class?
    A. K
    B. B
    C. C
    D. D

Answer - B
Reference - FFS, p 204

Chapter 8

41. Which of the following is one of the three basic components required for fire?
    A. An ignition source
    B. A catalyst
    C. Carbon
    D. Oxygen

Answer - D
Reference - FFS, p 205

42. Bromochlorodifluoromethane is a _____ agent.
    A. Halogenated
    B. Wet chemical
    C. Class D
    D. Multipurpose dry chemical

Answer - A
Reference - FFS, p 209

43. Which feature of some carbon dioxide extinguishers makes them dangerous for use on Class C fires?
    A. Loaded stream
    B. External cartridge
    C. Steel cylinder
    D. Metal horn

Answer - D
Reference - FFS, p 210

44. The weight of carbon dioxide is about _____ the weight of air.
    A. Half of
    B. Equal to
    C. One-and-a-half times
    D. Twice

Answer - C
Reference - FFS, p 207

45. For an extinguishing agent to be approved for use on energized electrical equipment, it must:
    A. Be electrically nonconductive
    B. Leave no residue
    C. Form a vapor barrier
    D. Be safe for use in a closed room

Answer - A
Reference - FFS, p 201

46. The use of Halon 1211 is strictly controlled because it is:
    A. Mutagenic
    B. Harmful to the environment
    C. A chemical asphyxiant
    D. Carcinogenic

Answer - B
Reference - FFS, p 209

47. Which class of fire involves energized electrical equipment?
    A. A
    B. B
    C. C
    D. D

Answer - C
Reference - FFS, p 201

48. A Class K agent's effect on the fuel is known as:
    A. Emulsification
    B. Saponification
    C. Dissolution
    D. Hydrolyzation

Answer - B
Reference - FFS, p 209

49. The traditional symbol for a Class D fire extinguisher is a(n):
    A. Orange circle
    B. Blue square
    C. Yellow star
    D. Green triangle

Answer - C
Reference - FFS, p 203

50. What is the difference between dry powder and dry chemical extinguishing agents?
    A. "Dry powder" and "dry chemical" are both terms for the same class of agents.
    B. A dry powder is compatible with foam; a dry chemical is not.
    C. A dry powder is harmful to the environment; a dry chemical is not.
    D. Each is rated for a different class of fire.

Answer - D
Reference - FFS, p 215

51. Which is a polar solvent?
    A. Diesel fuel
    B. Alcohol
    C. Jet fuel
    D. Kerosene

Answer - B
Reference - FFS, p 208

Notes on Portable Fire Extinguishers

1. Class A (symbol - green triangle, pictograph - burning trash can and campfire) - water and foam
2. Class B (symbol - red square, pictograph - burning gas can) - foam
3. Class C (symbol - blue circle, pictograph - burning electrical cord and outlet) - dry chemicals or carbon dioxide
4. Class D (symbol - yellow diamond, pictograph - none) - dry powder
5. Class K (symbol - none, pictograph - burning cooking skillet)

Chapter 9
Firefighter Tools and Equipment

1. Which statement about the use of power saws is correct?
    A. Power saws can be hard to start.
    B. Power saws are easy to operate.
    C. Power saws are more portable than hand saws.
    D. Power saws increase operator fatigue.

Answer - A
Reference - FFS, p 246

2. Which tool is a hand-powered hydraulic spreader tool?
    A. Spanner
    B. Kelly
    C. Rabbet
    D. Pivot

Answer - C
Reference - FFS, p 242

3. Which tool is commonly used for debris removal?
    A. Hux
    B. Pulaski
    C. Shovel
    D. Pike pole

Answer - C
Reference - FFS, p 251

4. Which tool is used to pull down a ceiling?
    A. Pike pole
    B. K tool
    C. Rabbet tool
    D. Kelly tool

Answer - A
Reference - FFS, p 240

Chapter 9

5. What does the "R" stand for in "RIC"?
   A. Responder
   B. Response
   C. Rescue
   D. Rapid

Answer – D. "RIC" is the rapid intervention crew. Their primary task is to rescue firefighters in trouble.
Reference - FFS, p 250

6. Which tool has a closed end and is used to tighten nuts or bolts?
   A. Adjustable
   B. Spanner
   C. Box-end
   D. Pipe

Answer - C
Reference - FFS, p 239

7. Which tool is classified as a prying/spreading tool?
   A. Spanner
   B. K tool
   C. Kelly tool
   D. Axe

Answer - C
Reference - FFS, p 241

8. The use of a fan to blow clean air into a structure and force fire gases out is known as _____ ventilation.
   A. Mechanical
   B. Positive pressure
   C. Horizontal
   D. Ejection

Answer – B. This improves the environment including decreasing heat and improving visibility, but can make things worse by supplying air to a ventilation-limited fire if poorly done. Ventilation should be done at the same time as putting water on the fire.
Reference - FFS, p 251

9. What is the most common use for a hydraulic spreader?
   A. Lifting heavy objects
   B. Vehicle stabilization
   C. Shoring
   D. Vehicle extrication

Answer - D
Reference - FFS, p 242

10. The use of a hand tool should be followed by:
    A. testing
    B. sharpening
    C. weighing
    D. documentation

Answer - D
Reference - FFS, p 252

11. Rotating tools are used to assemble parts that are connected by which means?
    A. Welds
    B. Nails
    C. Rivets
    D. Threaded fasteners

Answer - D
Reference - FFS, p 238

12. Which saw is designed for cutting curves into wood?
    A. Coping
    B. Carpenter's handsaw
    C. Hacksaw
    D. Fret

Answer - A
Reference - FFS, p 244

Chapter 9

13. Which statement about the use of existing roof openings for vertical ventilation is correct?
    A. Existing roof openings are generally impractical to force open.
    B. Existing roof openings should be used whenever possible.
    C. No additional openings should be cut in a roof that has preexisting openings.
    D. Existing roof openings are generally too small to be useful.

Answer - B
Reference - FFS, p 251

14. Which tool is classified as a rotating tool?
    A. Pike pole
    B. Screwdriver
    C. Halligan
    D. Pry bar

Answer - B
Reference - FFS, p 239

15. The bar of a pry bar acts as a _____ to multiply the amount of force that can be applied.
    A. Fulcrum
    B. Ratchet
    C. Pivot
    D. Lever

Answer - D
Reference - FFS, p 241

16. Using a spring-loaded center punch to break tempered automobile glass results in _____.
    A. Irregular pieces of glass of varying sizes and shapes
    B. A sheet of spidered glass
    C. Many small, uniform-sized pieces of glass
    D. Large, sharp-edged shards of glass

Answer - C
Reference - FFS, p 244

17. Which statement about painting hand tools is correct?
    A. Rust-inhibiting paint should be applied to the nonworking surfaces of metal tools.
    B. Paint will extend the life of wood handles.
    C. Paint will evolve flammable vapors in a fire environment.
    D. The use of paint on tools can hide defects or damage.

Answer - D
Reference - FFS, p 252

18. A short-handled hammer with a round head is called a:
    A. Sledge
    B. Maul
    C. Mallet
    D. Trip

Answer – C
Reference - FFS, p 242

19. What qualifies a hammer as a sledgehammer?
    A. It is long and heavy enough to require the use of both hands.
    B. It has a pick on one side of the head.
    C. The head weighs at least 6 pounds.
    D. The head is round.

Answer - A
Reference - FFS, p 242

20. Which component is part of a Halligan tool?
    A. Cutting blade
    B. Spring-loaded hook
    C. Forked claw
    D. Hydrant spanner

Answer - C
Reference - FFS, p 241

Chapter 9

21. Which two tools are often used in combination to pry a door open?
    A. Sledgehammer and pick-head axe
    B. Flat-head axe and Halligan tool
    C. K tool and flat-head screwdriver
    D. Pry bar and wooden wedge

Answer – B. Combined, the flat head axe and the Halligan tool are called "the irons." They are frequently used for forced entry through doors.
Reference - FFS, p 243

22. Which tool is commonly used in interior search and rescue?
    A. Thermal imaging device
    B. Cribbing/shoring
    C. Acoustic detection device
    D. Multi-gas detector

Answer - A
Reference - FFS, p 250

23. What is the rabbet tool used for?
    A. Forcing open a locked door
    B. Making a temporary repair to a burst hose
    C. Opening a hydrant
    D. Anchoring a rope

Answer - A
Reference - FFS, p 242

24. The Halligan is classified as a _____ tool.
    A. Prying/spreading
    B. Striking
    C. Cutting
    D. Pushing/pulling

Answer - A
Reference - FFS, p 241

25. How often should power equipment be tested?
    A. Daily
    B. Frequently
    C. Weekly
    D. Monthly

Answer - B
Reference - FFS, p 253

26. Which type of saw is most used in vehicle extrication?
    A. Rotary
    B. Chain
    C. Circular
    D. Reciprocating

Answer - D
Reference - FFS, p 247

27. Which mechanical device is needed to accomplish negative-pressure ventilation?
    A. Chainsaw
    B. Fan
    C. Fog stream
    D. Draft curtain

Answer - B
Reference - FFS, p 251

28. What does the "I" stand for in "RIC"?
    A. Intervention
    B. Intermediate
    C. Immediate
    D. Initial

Answer – A. As noted earlier, RIC stands for "Rapid Intervention Crew."
Reference - FFS, p 250

Chapter 9

29. Which tool is a short pike pole designed for use in tight spaces?
    A. Closet hook
    B. K tool
    C. Plaster hook
    D. Clemens hook

Answer - A
Reference - FFS, p 240

30. A specialized tool for tightening or loosening hose couplings is the wrench:
    A. strap
    B. hose
    C. spanner
    D. ring

Answer - C
Reference - FFS, p 239

31. Which guide should be used for the care and inspection of power tools?
    A. The applicable NFPA standard
    B. The fire agency's SOPs
    C. The manufacturer's instructions
    D. It varies with the type of tool

Answer - C
Reference - FFS, p 252

32. What is one of the basic hand tools that an interior search and rescue team should carry?
    A. Long pike pole
    B. Prying tool
    C. Reciprocating saw
    D. Rotating tool

Answer - B
Reference - FFS, p 249

33. Which tool is designed to pull a lock cylinder out of a door?
    A. Rabbet tool
    B. Huxbar
    C. K tool
    D. Lock cutter

Answer - C
Reference - FFS, p 240

34. Which statement best describes the process of overhaul?
    A. Overhaul ensures that all rema<u>ining</u> fire is discovered and extinguished after the main fire has been knocked down.
    B. Actions are taken to protect property from preventable smoke, fire, and water damage.
    C. Overhaul includes demobilization and the release of resources from the scene.
    D. Overhaul focuses on preservation of evidence, investigation, and determination of fire cause and origin.

Answer - A
Reference - FFS, p 251

35. For which application would the use of a pick-head axe be incorrect?
    A. Ventilating a roof
    B. Prying up boards
    C. Striking another tool
    D. Puncturing a door

Answer – C. The pick-head axe has a pick opposite the axe head instead of a flat surface like a regular axe has.
Reference - FFS, p 243

36. What is one of the basic types of powered hydraulic tools used in rescue incidents?
    A. Shears/cutters
    B. Air impact wrench
    C. Struts
    D. Come along

Answer – A
Reference - FFS, p 241

Chapter 9

Notes on Firefighter Tools and Equipment

1. Striking - hammer, mallet, sledgehammer, maul, flat head axe, pick head axe, battering ram, chisel, spring loaded center punch
2. Prying/spreading - claw bar, crowbar, flat bar, Halligan tool, Hux bar, Kelly tool, hydraulic spreader, Rabbet tool
3. Cutting - seat belt cutter, bolt cutter, hack saw, carpenter's hand saw, coping saw, keyhole saw, reciprocating saw, rotating saw
4. Pushing/pulling - ceiling hook, Clemens hook, drywall hook, multipurpose hook, plaster hook, Roofman's hook, San Francisco hook, K tool (pull lock out of door)
5. Rotating - screwdrivers, wrenches, pliers, rachets and sockets
6. Special tools - hand light, thermal imaging device, SCBA, portable lighting, litter, or patient transport device

Response phases
1. Response and size up
2. Forcible entry
3. Search and rescue - four-man team, multiple tools
4. Interior firefighting
5. Overhaul
6. Salvage

Chapter 10
Ropes and Knots

1. Compared to a natural fiber rope, a synthetic fiber rope:
    A. Has a smaller diameter than a natural fiber rope of equal strength?
    B. Is weakened to a lesser degree by knots
    C. Is more susceptible to heat damage
    D. Is less susceptible to damage from acid or alkali exposure

Answer – A
Reference - FFS, p 262

2. Which knot would typically be used to attach a rope to a tree or pole?
    A. Square knot
    B. Bowline on a bight
    C. Figure eight on a bight
    D. Clove hitch

Answer - D
Reference - FFS, p 272

3. Which class of harness is used to support a fire fighter being raised or lowered on a life safety rope?
    A. I
    B. II
    C. III
    D. IV

Answer – C. Class I is a body belt (escape and ladder belt), class II is a seat harness, class III is a full body harness, and class IV is a suspension belt.
Reference - FFS, p 266

4. Which question is important to consider when inspecting life safety ropes?
    A. Has the rope ever been under load?
    B. How long has the rope been in storage?
    C. Has the rope been subject to shock loading?
    D. Has the rope been exposed to sunlight?

Answer – C. Shock loading occurs when someone or something heavy falls while attached to the rope. A life safety rope becomes a utility rope after one fall.
Reference - FFS, p 269

Chapter 10

5. What is the second most common synthetic fiber used for life safety ropes?
   A. Polyester
   B. Rayon
   C. Monoester
   D. Polypropylene

Answer – A. Nylon is first, polyester second, and polypropylene third. Polypropylene does not absorb water, so it is often used for water rescues.
Reference - FFS, p 263

6. Which family of knots is used primarily to attach a rope around an object?
   A. Hitches
   B. Bends
   C. Bights
   D. Loops

Answer - A
Reference - FFS, p 271

7. Which NFPA standard covers the criteria for design, construction, and performance of life safety rope and related equipment?
   A. 1981
   B. 1982
   C. 1983
   D. 1984

Answer - C
Reference - FFS, p 260

8. What is a defining characteristic of utility rope?
   A. It is de-rated or expired rescue rope.
   B. It must not be used to support the weight of a person.
   C. It features natural fiber construction.
   D. It has a minimum breaking strength of 300 lb (135 kg).

Answer - B
Reference - FFS, p 261

9. Which natural fiber is commonly used to make ropes?
   A. Manila
   B. Wool
   C. Horsehair
   D. Coir

Answer - A
Reference - FFS, p 262

10. Which fiber is commonly used in life safety rope?
    A. Sisal
    B. Rayon
    C. Nylon
    D. Olefin

Answer - C
Reference - FFS, p 263

11. What is formed by making a circle in a rope?
    A. Bight
    B. Snub
    C. Loop
    D. Coil

Answer - C
Reference - FFS, p 271

12. The term for a rope that is suddenly put under unusual tension is _____ loading.
    A. Impact
    B. Drop
    C. Tensile
    D. Shock

Answer - D
Reference - FFS, p 268

Chapter 10

13. A rope is attached to a ladder for hoisting using a(n):
    A. Clove hitch
    B. Bowline
    C. Figure eight on a bight
    D. Overhand safety

Answer - C
Reference - FFS, p 279

14. Which part of a rope is used for hoisting?
    A. Running end
    B. Working end
    C. Standing part
    D. Free end

Answer – A
Reference - FFS, p 271

15. What is the preferred type for rope for rescue operations?
    A. Braided
    B. Twisted
    C. Plaited
    D. Kernmantle

Answer - D
Reference - FFS, p 264

16. Which method of construction is required for life safety rope?
    A. Plaited
    B. Woven
    C. Block creel
    D. Solid braid

Answer - C
Reference - FFS, p 263

Ropes and Knots

17. Which type of harness is used in the fire service?
    A. Climbing
    B. Web
    C. Utility
    D. Full Body

Answer - D
Reference - FFS, p 266

18. Which statement about natural fiber ropes is correct?
    A. Natural fiber ropes are no longer approved for fire service use.
    B. Natural fiber ropes absorb less water than synthetic ropes.
    C. Some natural fiber ropes are approved for life-safety use.
    D. Natural fiber ropes deteriorate even if stored properly.

Answer - D
Reference - FFS, p 262

19. What is one of the three primary classifications of rope based on function?
    A. Static
    B. Rigging
    C. Utility
    D. Rescue

Answer – C. Types of rope include life safety, escape, and utility.
Reference - FFS, p 260

20. For which application is dynamic rope especially well suited?
    A. Rescue
    B. Mountaineering
    C. Hoisting
    D. Static loads

Answer - B
Reference - FFS, p 265

Chapter 10

21. Which knot is frequently used to secure the end of the rope to an anchor point?
    A. Overhand safety
    B. Becket bend
    C. Bowline
    D. Square

Answer - C
Reference - FFS, p 279

22. What is a common cause of deterioration in natural fiber ropes?
    A. Storage in a low-humidity environment
    B. Mildew
    C. Storage in a rope bag
    D. Infrequent use

Answer - B
Reference - FFS, p 262

23. Which method is usually recommended for drying ropes?
    A. A laundry dryer
    B. A hose dryer
    C. Air drying
    D. Direct sunlight

Answer - C
Reference - FFS, p 268

24. Which kind of rescue takes place in a location such as a tank, silo, underground electrical vault, or storm drain?
    A. Confined space
    B. Trench
    C. Technical
    D. Urban search and rescue

Answer - A
Reference - FFS, p 267

25. What is another term for a safety knot?
    A. Rescue knot
    B. Finishing knot
    C. Overhand knot
    D. Half hitch

Answer - A
Reference - FFS, p 271

26. Which of the following is a commonly used device in rope rescue operations?
    A. Carabiner
    B. Jake plate
    C. Power winch
    D. Come along

Answer - A
Reference - FFS, p 265

27. Natural fiber ropes are created using which type of construction?
    A. Twisted
    B. Braid-on-braid
    C. Kernmantle
    D. Plaited

Answer - A
Reference - FFS, p 262

28. The individual fibers of a natural fiber ropes are twisted together to form a _____.
    A. Twill
    B. Plait
    C. Strand
    D. Creel

Answer - C
Reference - FFS, p 262

29. Which of the following is one of the four parts of the maintenance formula for ropes?
   A. Store
   B. Dry
   C. Coil
   D. Feel

Answer – A. Care, Clean, Inspect and Store are the four parts.
Reference - FFS, p 268

30. What is the term for a piece of rescue equipment worn by a person to secure that individual to a rope?
   A. Cam-lock
   B. Tie-in
   C. Harness
   D. Ladder belt

Answer - C
Reference - FFS, p 266

31. Which of the following is a second line attached to a rescuer that serves as a backup if the main line fails?
   A. Tag
   B. Lifeline
   C. Tether
   D. Belay

Answer - D
Reference - FFS, p 267

32. What is formed by making a loop in a rope and then bringing the two ends of the rope parallel to each other?
   A. Eye
   B. Cinch
   C. Round turn
   D. Bend

Answer - C
Reference - FFS, p 271

33. What is another term for a sheet bend?
    A. Lark's foot
    B. Round turn
    C. Becket bend
    D. Water knot

Answer – C. A water knot is used to tie webbing together.
Reference - FFS, p 279

34. What is a common sign of damage to a kernmantle rope?
    A. Discoloration
    B. Loose or twisted sheath
    C. Depressions in the kern
    D. Fuzziness of the mantle

Answer - C
Reference - FFS, p 269

35. What is formed by reversing the direction of a rope to form a "U" bend with two parallel ends?
    A. Loop
    B. Bend
    C. Round turn
    D. Bight

Answer - D
Reference - FFS, p 271

36. A figure eight on a bight is used to:
    A. Create a secure loop at the working end
    B. Wrap a loop around an object
    C. Attach a rope to an eye or ring
    D. Join two ropes together

Answer - C
Reference - FFS, p 279

Chapter 10

37. Which type of rope consists of individual strands twisted together?
   A. Braided
   B. Laid
   C. Twine
   D. Twisted

Answer - D
Reference - FFS, p 262

38. Which knot component is part of a clove hitch?
   A. Round turn
   B. Loop
   C. Follow-though
   D. Bight

Answer - B
Reference - FFS, p 273

39. Which knot is typically used to tie together two ropes of unequal size?
   A. Bowline
   B. Half hitch
   C. Square
   D. Becket bend

Answer - D
Reference - FFS, p 279

40. Which item is necessary to include in a life safety rope's documentation?
   A. History of use
   B. Vendor
   C. Recommended storage method
   D. Expiration date

Answer - A
Reference - FFS, p 270

Ropes and Knots

41. What kind of line should be attached to the bottom of the ladder to help control it when hoisting a ladder?
   A. Tag
   B. Safety
   C. Guy
   D. Spring

Answer - A
Reference - FFS, p 289

42. Which class of harness is used to support a fire fighter in a rescue situation?
   A. I
   B. II
   C. III
   D. IV

Answer – B
Reference - FFS, p 266

43. A carabiner is a type of device:
   A. Connecting
   B. Anchoring
   C. Braking
   D. Ascending

Answer – A
Reference - FFS, p 266

44. Which knot is used to keep the hoisting rope aligned with the handle of a tool being hoisted?
   A. Half sheepshank
   B. Directional figure eight
   C. Half hitch
   D. Overhand

Answer - C
Reference - FFS, p 272

Chapter 10

45. Prolonged exposure to _____ light can damage synthetic ropes.
   A. Ultraviolet
   B. Infrared
   C. Polarized
   D. Spectral

Answer - A
Reference - FFS, p 263

Notes on Rope and Knots

Type of Rope
1. Life safety - synthetic fibers only, kernmantle type, size 11-16 mm, block creel construction
2. Utility - natural or synthetic fibers, twisted or braided,
3. Escape - single use life safety rope for an individual firefighter.
4. Search rope - kernmantle, fire resistant, each search and rescue firefighter is hooked in and the first rescuer holds the bag and feeds the rope out

Chapter 11
Response and Size Up

1. When is a natural gas shut-off valve in the closed position?
   A. When the handle is at a right angle to the pipe
   B. When the stem is fully rotated inward
   C. When the bar is parallel to the pipe
   D. When the valve handle is fully rotated clockwise

Answer - A
Reference - FFS, p 306

2. A gas valve that has been shut off may be reopened:
   A. After completion of overhaul
   B. If the fire was confined to room contents only
   C. After the system has been inspected by a qualified person
   D. Upon restoration of electrical power

Answer - C
Reference - FFS, p 306

3. In a fire response, which goal has the highest priority?
   A. Save lives
   B. Protecting building contents
   C. Preventing spread of fire to exposures
   D. Extinguishing the fire

Answer - A
Reference - FFS, p 311

4. Fire fighters attack the fire with heavy streams from outside the fire building during a(n) attack:
   A. Perimeter
   B. Indirect
   C. Offensive
   D. Defensive

Answer - D
Reference - FFS, p 313

Chapter 11

5. What is the second priority in basic fire-ground objectives?
   A. Salvage
   B. Exposure protection
   C. Extinguishment
   D. Confinement

Answer - B
Reference - FFS, p 311

6. Which characteristic is associated with modern lightweight construction techniques?
   A. Higher dead load
   B. A more air-tight structure
   C. Greater susceptibility to collapse
   D. Unstopped stud bays

Answer - C
Reference - FFS, p 308

7. Which construction feature of older buildings provides a path for rapid spread of fire?
   A. Unreinforced masonry
   B. Platform construction
   C. Lath and plaster interior finish
   D. Balloon-frame construction

Answer - D
Reference - FFS, p 308

8. The incident commander outlines the steps needed to bring an incident under control in the:
   A. Situation status report
   B. Incident action plan
   C. Initial report
   D. Report on conditions

Answer - B
Reference - FFS, p 311

9. In which situation should utility company personnel be called to interrupt power from a remote location?
    A. Wires outside the fire building are damaged
    B. Multiple hose lines are in use
    C. The building houses multiple living units
    D. Occupants are non- or semi-ambulatory

Answer - A
Reference - FFS, p 305

10. At a traffic accident scene, apparatus should be _____.
    A. Parked as far to the right as possible
    B. Parked in the left-hand lane immediately adjacent to the scene
    C. Positioned on the opposite side of the scene as the oncoming traffic
    D. Positioned to create a barrier between the oncoming traffic and the scene

Answer - D
Reference - FFS, p 304

11. When performing size-up, which question can most reliably be answered based on the time of day?
    A. Is the building occupied?
    B. Is the alarm a result of system malfunction?
    C. Was the fire intentionally set?
    D. Is the fire threatening exposures?

Answer - A
Reference - FFS, p 308

12. Which term means the evaluation of structure fire conditions to determine if occupants could be alive?
    A. Size-up
    B. Survivability profiling
    C. Risk management
    D. Triage

Answer - B
Reference - FFS, p 312

Chapter 11

13. What is the term for the process of finding and completely extinguishing any remaining pockets of fire?
    A. Salvage
    B. Overhaul
    C. Mop-up
    D. Investigation

Answer - B
Reference - FFS, p 314

14. Which building feature would create the greatest challenge for fire fighters in gaining access to trapped victims?
    A. Hung acoustic ceilings
    B. Security bars on windows
    C. Solid-core doors
    D. Self-closing fire doors

Answer - B
Reference - FFS, p 308

15. The priorities of the basic five fire-ground objectives are _____.
    A. Separate and exclusive
    B. Not separate and not exclusive
    C. Separate but not exclusive
    D. Not separate but exclusive

Answer - B
Reference - FFS, p 311

16. The upper temperature limit in which people can survive is _____.
    A. 212^0F (100^0 C)
    B. 270^0F (132^0 C)
    C. 318^0F (158^0 C)
    D. 350^0F (176^0 C)

Answer – A. Water boils at 212^0F, including the water which constitutes well over half of the human body weight.
Reference - FFS, p 312

17. How much risk should fire fighters take to attempt to recover a victim who has no chance of surviving?
    A. None
    B. A little
    C. A lot
    D. Unlimited

Answer - A
Reference - FFS, p 312

18. Who first developed the RECEO tactical model?
    A. Lloyd Layman
    B. Alan Brunacini
    C. John Norman
    D. James Smith

Answer - A
Reference - FFS, p 312

19. When should fire fighters don their PPE?
    A. Prior to mounting the apparatus
    B. Immediately upon mounting the apparatus
    C. Enroute to the scene of the incident
    D. Upon arrival at the scene

Answer - A
Reference - FFS, p 301

20. What is a common indicator of hidden fire burning within a wall?
    A. Deformation
    B. Crackling sounds
    C. Blistering paint
    D. Charring of gypsum board

Answer - C
Reference - FFS, p 309

21. Fire that is spreading to an exposure is:
    A. Extending
    B. Crowning
    C. Running
    D. Free burning

Answer - A
Reference - FFS, p 313

22. When performing size-up, what is the most reliable source of facts about a structure?
    A. Eyewitness accounts
    B. Reporting party information
    C. A preincident plan
    D. Initial report

Answer - C
Reference - FFS, p 308

23. Which location presents the most immediate life-safety hazard for an apartment fire?
    A. The apartment directly underneath the fire
    B. The apartments adjacent to the fire
    C. The uppermost floor of the building
    D. The apartment directly above the fire

Answer – D
Reference - FFS, p 309

24. It is of particular importance to control utilities prior to:
    A. Setting up positive-pressure ventilation
    B. Opening walls
    C. Beginning salvage operations
    D. Ventilating the roof

Answer - B
Reference - FFS, p 305

Response and Size Up

25. What is a critical factor to consider when evaluating the potential for collapse of a burning structure?
    A. Size of the collapse zone
    B. Reflex time
    C. Weather conditions
    D. How long it has been burning

Answer - D
Reference - FFS, p 310

26. Which exemptions or privileges do fire fighters have when responding to an emergency in their personal vehicles?
    A. The same as emergency vehicles
    B. It varies by jurisdiction
    C. None; they are treated just like any other private car
    D. They are permitted to regard stoplights as stop signs

Answer - B
Reference - FFS, p 303

27. Freelancing is considered:
    A. Necessary
    B. Unacceptable
    C. Commendable
    D. Responsible

Answer - B
Reference - FFS, p 304

28. Which statement best summarizes an apparatus operator's legal responsibility for the safe operation of that vehicle?
    A. The operator is not legally responsible for the safe operation of the vehicle; instead, legal responsibility is borne by the agency.
    B. The operator is legally responsible for the safe operation of the vehicle at all times.
    C. The operator is legally exempt from liability during an emergency response.
    D. The operator is not legally responsible for the safe operation of the vehicle but is considered morally responsible.

Answer - B
Reference - FFS, p 303

Chapter 11

29. During operations in traffic areas, lane and street closures should be performed according to:
   A. Department SOP
   B. NFPA standard
   C. State vehicle code
   D. Advice of law enforcement personnel

Answer - A
Reference - FFS, p 304

30. Of the basic fire-ground objectives, which item is third in order of priority?
   A. Rescue victims
   B. Extinguish the fire
   C. Confine the fire
   D. Protect exposures

Answer – C. The priorities are Save Lives, Protect Exposures, Confine the Fire, Extinguish the Fire, and Salvage Property/Overhaul the Fire
Reference - FFS, p 311

31. What is the first step in the process of response?
   A. Checking PPE
   B. Mounting the apparatus
   C. Determining the route of travel
   D. Belting in

Answer - A
Reference - FFS, p 300

32. Taking action without orders or regard for SOPs is known as:
   A. Initiative
   B. Improvisation
   C. Freelancing
   D. Independent action

Answer - C
Reference - FFS, p 304

Response and Size Up

33. An event or outcome that is predicted based on known facts, common sense, and previous experience is a _____.
    A. Fact
    B. Possibility
    C. Probability
    D. Projection

Answer - C
Reference - FFS, p 309

34. As an incident progresses, what is an additional factor to be evaluated in the ongoing size-up?
    A. Establishment of an overall goal for the incident
    B. Actions that can be safely accomplished
    C. Additional resources needed
    D. The effectiveness of the initial plan

Answer - D
Reference - FFS, p 306

35. What do fire departments commonly use to manage incidents that require more resources than are immediately available?
    A. Isolation and withdrawal policies
    B. A regional emergency operations center
    C. Mutual aid agreements
    D. A local incident management system

Answer - C
Reference - FFS, p 311

36. Which of the following is one of a fire department's two basic resources?
    A. Organization
    B. Training
    C. Apparatus
    D. Leadership

Answer – C. The two basic resources are personnel and apparatuses.
Reference - FFS, p 311

Chapter 11

37. Which process enables the incident commander to determine which resources will be needed to control the situation?
   A. Personnel accountability
   B. Size-up
   C. Preincident planning
   D. Chain of command

Answer - B
Reference - FFS, p 306

38. How is natural gas usually delivered?
   A. From a large outdoor cylinder or tank
   B. Through underground pipes
   C. In portable cylinders
   D. As a liquefied gas

Answer - B
Reference - FFS, p 306

39. What is the first step in making plans to manage an emergency incident?
   A. Perform size-up
   B. Establish personnel accountability
   C. Establish command
   D. Transmit/receive the initial report

Answer - A
Reference - FFS, p 306

40. Which term describes operations undertaken to prevent avoidable property loss?
   A. Salvage
   B. Overhaul
   C. Recovery
   D. Property conservation

Answer - A
Reference - FFS, p 314

Notes on Response and Size Up

Brief description of the incident - paint a picture for incoming units

Dispatch (prearrival)
1. Initial size up begins when you are toned.
2. More reliable information if multiple calls have been received.
3. Location of incident, type of emergency, units due to respond

Officer enroute (right front - occupant)
1. Get as much info as possible enroute from dispatch and others
2. Make strategic game plan, collect accountability tags, give out assignments
3. Enroute report - road (dry, water, snow, ice, obstacles) and traffic conditions, best route to incident
4. Park so that you can see two or even three sides of building.
5. On arrival at scene - Size up, establish command, do a 360^0 walk around. Initial and secondary size up.
6. After 360^0, establish a command post and assess the fire ground

Initial on scene radio report
1. Unit/truck on scene – example "Raleigh control, Station 102 Engine 1"
2. Area description - commercial, industrial, residential, rural, suburban, urban, strip mall, church, hydrants, water supply
3. Building description - size, occupancy (people present), use, stories, construction (ranch, farmhouse, balloon), basement, handicapped ramp, outside stairs, chimney
4. Vehicle description - damage (heavy, moderate, light), fire (location, extent), occupancy, entrapment (unknown), injuries (unknown), fuel spill, air bags (unknown, deployed), approach at 45 degrees (beware shock absorber explosion)
5. Smoke conditions - color (black, gray, brown, white), volume (thick, medium, small)
6. Fire conditions - room and contents, attic (no fire in windows), development (fully, through the roof, all areas), color of smoke
7. Sides of building - A - front, B - clockwise from front, C - rear, D - clockwise from rear
8. Hazards - Electrical, gas, HAZMAT, collapse, power (off, on), fuel tanks (propane, diesel, LNG, gasoline), power lines
9. Action plan - investigative (what is going on?), offensive (going in), defensive (surround and drown), transitional (knock fire down a little, then go in). Do not go from defensive to offensive.
10. If likelihood of many people - evacuate
11. Additional resources needed - water, people (qualifications, health)

Chapter 11

12. Who is in command?

Assigning units
1. Interior attack
2. Ventilation
3. RIT - Rescue team (mayday call, man down)
4. Water supply
5. Search

Secondary size up is an ongoing evaluation of the incident. Size up structure, hazards, manpower, and other resources. How is your team doing?

Transferring command
1. When a higher-ranking officer arrives on scene
2. Done face to face, including complete briefing on situation with all of the information noted above
3. Broadcast transfer of command over the radio so that everyone knows the change in situation
4. Dispatch must be advised of transfer

Radio
1. Attack channel BVFD - Tac 1 or Tab 2 for communication
2. County channel - Raleigh County Fire
3. Fire Ground 1 for operations

Terminating command - Last in, first out

Notes on Thermal Imaging in Fire Service

Purpose
1. Looking for people
2. Looking for fire hot spots to attack
3. Avoid getting lost inside a building
4. Get an idea of temperatures in an area to minimize exposure
5. Look for hot spots and cold spots (cold spots for rescue and escape)

Line of Duty Deaths (LODD)
1. IDLH - Immediate danger to life and health
2. Captain Jeff Bowen, 28 July 2011, Asheville NC - got lost and ran out of air in a cube farm in a medical office building
3. Detroit MI, 3 Cleveland Ave - 2016

118

4. Shane Daughtee, 27 January 2007, Hamilton County TN, - basement fire, TIC was not used
5. Project Mayday - fall into or trapped in basement 746 cases, TIC used during 360 incidents (27%)

Thermal Imaging Camera (TIC) sees radiated heat from surfaces.

A Different Fire Environment
1. Modern materials and construction
2. Pyrolysis (chemical decomposition of material caused by heat) begins at 300-400 degrees in natural products but 180 degrees for synthetics.
3. Synthetics - increased rate of heat release, oxygen consumption, and volatile environments
4. Homes - energy efficient, "tight"
5. Fires that we fight are different than fires that we train in.

Burn Scale (medical effects in degrees Fahrenheit)
1. Protein coagulation - 162 (third degree burn)
2. Numbness - 140
3. Second degree burn - 131
4. Severe pain - 125
5. Moderate pain - 118
6. Pain threshold - 113

Fire gear
1. Best bunker gear protects against 573 degrees for 17 seconds
2. Ten-year shelf life on turn out gear
3. Damage to fire gear occurs much later than damage to humans inside the fire gear.
4. Mask - fails at 446 degrees
5. Radio - fails at 320 degrees
6. Hose lines - fail 400-485 degrees even while flowing water.
7. It is hotter than we realize.

Victims and unprotected others
1. Tracheal failure at 180-degree air temperatures for 20 seconds
2. PPE thermal limits are designed to protect the firefighter (FF) to a tested limit, but our tactics do not consider these limits when placing the FF into IDLH environments.

Low staffing results in less searching
FFs have higher rates of all kinds of cancer than the general population.

Chapter 11

Modes
1. High sensitivity - no green triangle in upper left-hand corner, up to 300 degrees, grayscale, higher resolution, better for search
2. Low sensitivity - green triangle in upper left-hand corner, 34% of the image over 300 degrees, colorized (can seeing varying levels of heat)
3. Some cameras have medium mode sensitivity also.
4. Majority of cameras are not NFPA certified

TICs confirm things (high specificity), they do not rule them out (low sensitivity).

Using a TIC
1. Use with firefighter behind nozzle holder
2. Field of view differs vertically and horizontally depending upon grip.
3. Scanning pattern - low, middle, high moving across the room

Emissivity
1. Ability of an obj4ct to emit thermal radiation.
2. Lower emissivity with generally shinier objects, but they do not allow for accurate temperature readings. If looking at a window, mirror, or stainless-steel kitchen, fire may be reflected from somewhere else.

Types of cameras
1. Situational awareness - $500-$700, thermal sensor lower resolutions, less than 30 HZ (usually 10 or 15), thermal sensitivity over 100 mK, do not give enough information to make tactical decisions.
2. Decision making - $7000 - $9000, thermal sensor higher resolution, 60 HZ. larger display size, thermal sensitivity less than 30 mK.
3. Scott Sight - mask mounted situational awareness camera.

Application of TICs
1. Enhances but does not replace the situation size up.
2. May be unreliable in the floor above a fire
3. Cannot comment on structural stability
4. Slow down - take seconds, save minutes
5. Ensure a full scan - every portion of the structure. Walk with normal observations. Use camera for full scan at each corner while standing still.
6. Look inside open doors - victims are usually found near doors.
7. Learn to recognize normal.

8. Thermal bridges - objects which allow for greater heat transfer (conduction) than the surrounding materials. Eaves, windows, doors, areas of penetration from plumbing, electrical, etc.
9. First heat signature will be around the door or window.
10. If you get a heat signature on a doorknob, do not touch it. Doorknobs are shiny and do not seem hot until they are really hot.
11. Scan the whole room
12. Manually (hands on) search of beds, cribs, and places where people might be found.
13. Victims in a fire are usually colder than the rest of the environment and therefore are usually cold spots on the TIC.

Firefighterrescuesurvey.com
1. 75.6% of the time when a firefighter needs rescue, it is a low visibility environment.
2. TIC is used only 39% of the time in these circumstances

Chapter 12
Forcible Entry

1. What is the quickest way to force entry through a security roll-up door?
    A. Cut the door with a torch or saw
    B. Pry the latch bar away from the keeper
    C. Pry upward from the bottom of the door
    D. Cut the latch bar with a rotary saw

Answer - A
Reference - FFS, p 331

2. Which tool is specifically designed to open double doors equipped with panic bars?
    A. Slim Jim
    B. J tool
    C. Barfly
    D. Key tool

Answer - B
Reference - FFS, p 325

3. Which type of glass is normally used in automobile side and rear windows?
    A. Annealed
    B. Polycarbonate
    C. Laminated
    D. Tempered

Answer - D
Reference - FFS, p 333

4. Which of the following is one of the four major categories of door locks?
    A. Deadbolt
    B. Recessed
    C. Cylindrical
    D. Tumbler

Answer - C
Reference - FFS, p 339

Forcible Entry

5. How many people are needed to use a battering ram?
   A. Two
   B. Two to four
   C. Four to six
   D. Six

Answer - B
Reference - FFS, p 322

6. Which tool can be used to unscrew a lock cylinder?
   A. Strap wrench
   B. Vise grips
   C. Channel locks
   D. Chain whip

Answer - B
Reference - FFS, p 343

7. Breaching of which type of wall is most likely to result in structural collapse?
   A. Partition
   B. Exterior
   C. Sleeper
   D. Bearing

Answer - D
Reference - FFS, p 344

8. What is the term for the transparent part of a window?
   A. Glass
   B. Glazing
   C. Lens
   D. Light

Answer - B
Reference - FFS, p 332

Chapter 12

9. How much damage is caused by forcing the locks on double-hung windows?
   A. None
   B. Minor
   C. Moderate
   D. Extensive

Answer – D
Reference - FFS, p 334

10. What is the U-shaped part of a padlock that locks into the padlock body?
    A. Latch
    B. Shackle
    C. Tongue
    D. Bow

Answer - B
Reference - FFS, p 325

11. Which tool combines an adz, a pick, and a claw?
    A. Halligan bar
    B. Pick-head axe
    C. Ram bar
    D. Clemens

Answer - A
Reference - FFS, p 323

12. Tool failure and possibly injury could result from attempting to cut with ordinary cutting tools.
    A. Masonry
    B. Case-hardened steel
    C. Proof coil
    D. Braided wire

Answer - B
Reference - FFS, p 324

13. To force an inward-opening door, which part of the Halligan bar is inserted between the stop and the jamb?
   A. Fork
   B. Adz
   C. Blade
   D. Pick

Answer - B
Reference - FFS, p 327

14. Which hazard should be of particular concern to fire fighters who are carrying long tools?
   A. Overhead wires
   B. Tight turns in corridors
   C. Self-closing doors
   D. Windows

Answer - A
Reference - FFS, p 321

15. Which statement about outward-opening doors is correct?
   A. These doors are typically found on residential structures.
   B. These doors can be identified by their exposed stiles.
   C. These doors are designed to facilitate exit.
   D. The hinges of these doors are not accessible.

Answer - C
Reference - FFS, p 328

16. A duck-billed lock breaker is used to:
   A. Displace a lock cylinder
   B. Force casement and double-hung windows
   C. Open a padlock
   D. Displace automotive door locks

Answer - C
Reference - FFS, p 325

Chapter 12

17. Which circular saw blade is susceptible to damage from gasoline vapors?
    A. All blades
    B. Masonry
    C. Wood
    D. Polycarbonate

Answer - B
Reference - FFS, p 324

18. Which type of glass is normally used in automobile windshields?
    A. Annealed
    B. Reinforced
    C. Laminated
    D. Tempered

Answer - C
Reference - FFS, p 333

19. What is the minimum acceptable level of protective equipment when conducting forcible entry during fire suppression operations?
    A. Helmet and eye protection
    B. Gloves and eye protection
    C. Full structural firefighting PPE
    D. Helmet, coat, and gloves

Answer - C
Reference - FFS, p 321

20. Which tool is inserted between an older-style latch and the door frame to force the latch back and open the door?
    A. J tool
    B. Shove knife
    C. Slim Jim
    D. Hack saw blade

Answer - B
Reference - FFS, p 325

21. What is one of the two styles of wooden door frames?
    A. Rabbet
    B. Finger-joint
    C. Ledge
    D. Bam

Answer – A. The two types are stopped and rabbeted.
Reference - FFS, p 327

22. Which tool is designed specifically to cut into a lock cylinder?
    A. Hux bar
    B. J tool
    C. K tool
    D. Pry axe

Answer - C
Reference - FFS, p 324

23. Ideally, when forcible entry is used, what should fire fighters do before leaving the scene?
    A. Make the occupant aware of the unsecured openings
    B. Take steps to secure the building
    C. Bring the matter to the attention of law enforcement personnel
    D. Photograph and document the damage

Answer - B
Reference - FFS, p 320

24. Which type of tool is a pick-head axe?
    A. Prying
    B. Combination
    C. Striking
    D. Cutting

Answer - C
Reference - FFS, p 324

25. Which type of door is typically used for entrance doors?
    A. Solid core
    B. Panel
    C. Ledge
    D. Hollow core

Answer - A
Reference - FFS, p 326

26. How are jalousie windows normally opened and closed?
    A. Sliding the sash within the frame
    B. Using a remote-operated electric motor
    C. Turning a small hand-crank
    D. Pulling the chain attached to the drum

Answer - C
Reference - FFS, p 336

27. Which tool is designed for both cutting and prying?
    A. Bam-bam
    B. Ram bar
    C. Halligan
    D. Pry axe

Answer - D
Reference - FFS, p 323

28. Where are the hinges placed on a casement window?
    A. Side
    B. Top
    C. Bottom
    D. Middle

Answer - A
Reference - FFS, p 337

Forcible Entry

29. Which type of cutting blade can be damaged by gasoline vapors?
    A. Carbide tip
    B. Wood
    C. Plastic
    D. Metal

Answer - D
Reference - FFS, p 322

30. Which tool is a small hydraulic spreader operated by a hand-powered pump?
    A. K tool
    B. Power bar
    C. Rabbit tool
    D. Ram bar

Answer - C
Reference - FFS, p 323

31. How is the length of bolt cutter handles related to the amount of cutting force that can be applied?
    A. The cutting force remains constant regardless of the handle's length
    B. The shorter the handle, the greater the cutting force
    C. The longer the handle, the greater the cutting force
    D. The cutting force varies with the jaw length

Answer - C
Reference - FFS, p 324

32. The Hux bar is designed primarily for:
    A. Striking
    B. Cutting
    C. Lifting
    D. Prying

Answer - D
Reference - FFS, p 323

Chapter 12

33. Tempered glass is about _____ as strong as regular glass.
   A. Half
   B. Equally
   C. Twice
   D. Four times

Answer - D
Reference - FFS, p 333

34. A silicon carbide composite circular saw blade is designed for use on:
   A. Masonry
   B. Steel
   C. Most metals
   D. A wide variety of materials

Answer - A
Reference - FFS, p 324

35. Which tool is best for breaching a floor?
   A. Rotary saw
   B. Air chisel
   C. Flat-head axe
   D. Reciprocating saw

Answer - A
Reference - FFS, p 346

Notes on Forcible Entry

Lock types
1. Cylinder - deadbolt, doorknob
2. Mortise - a mortise lock is set inside a door. Especially used in glass door frames
3. Rim locks - "night latch", lock mounted on inside surface of door, can be operated from one or both sides
4. Padlocks

Go into the last door used.

Tools
1. Traditional irons
2. Officer's tool - 18 inches max length

130

Forcible Entry

3. Wedge metal/wood
4. Bolt cutters
5. K12 saw
6. Jaws of Life

Unusual tools
1. 8 lb. axe
2. Maximus/Rex Halligan
3. Rex tool, S&D Rex tool (recommended)
4. Through the Lock (TTL) pliers
5. Mini-bolt cutters
6. J tool - good for panic door hardware, recommended
7. Duckbill lockbreaker
8. FE bag
9. Weedeater string, webbing, ribbon
10. Putty knife
11. JV tool
12. Framing square
13. Tape, rubber tubes
14. Sparrows long shot - recommended
15. Firefighter swipe tool
16. Channel locks, locking pliers
17. Bump keys
18. Wedges of different sizes
19. Dental picks

Size up
1. Occupancy
2. Lock and door type
3. Emergency
4. Escalation of damage

Residential
1. Cylinder locks
2. Added hardware
3. Special situations - prepper, hoarder, unused doors

Commercial
1. Mortise lock with pivoting deadbolt
2. Adams Rite - pivoting deadbolt, slam latch, Adams Rite bypass driver (goes through keyhole)

3. Panic hardware
4. Single door
5. Double door

Metal commercial door
1. Usually on C side
2. Often push bar

Escalation of damage
1. No damage
2. Little to no damage
3. Lock and door damage
4. Door frame

Lock in the handle suggests that panic hardware is present

Notes on Forcible Entry

Basic door construction
1. Door - solid (exterior doors), hollow (interior doors), made of wood, metal, or glass, inward and outward opening
2. Jamb - the frame
3. Hardware - handles, hinges,
4. Locking mechanism
5. Types include sliding and rotating

Chapter 13
Ladders

1. Before climbing a ladder, fire fighters should make sure it is:
   A. Chocked
   B. Blocked
   C. Unoccupied
   D. Heeled

Answer – D. Another firefighter secures the ladder by holding it steady applying one's weight to the underside.
Reference - FFS, p 367

2. What is the very top of a ladder called?
   A. Fly
   B. Top plate
   C. Claw
   D. Tip

Answer - D
Reference - FFS, p 357

3. For a ladder contacting the wall 20 ft (6 m) above the ground, the base should be ___ from the wall.
   A. 3 ft (1 m)
   B. 4 ft (1.2 m)
   C. 5 ft (1.5 m)
   D. 6 ft (1.8 m)

Answer - C
Reference - FFS, p 367

4. When is it acceptable to use a roof ladder as a free-hanging ladder?
   A. Never
   B. If the ladder will support the weight of only one person
   C. If the total supported weight will not exceed 500 lb.
   D. If the ladder was manufactured after 1993

Answer - A
Reference – FFS p.360

5. A ladder consisting of a single section is called a ladder.
   A. Ground
   B. Straight
   C. Roof
   D. Fly

Answer - B
Reference - FFS, p 360

6. A ladder belt or a leg lock should be used when:
   A. Moving an unconscious victim down a ladder
   B. Tying in either the fly or the butt
   C. Carrying equipment up or down the ladder
   D. Reaching or working from a ladder

Answer - D
Reference - FFS, p 368

7. Which part is specifically designed to prevent the beams of a wooden ladder from separating?
   A. Tie rod
   B. Protection plate
   C. Rung
   D. Spring bar

Answer - A
Reference - FFS, p 357

8. When raising a ladder, it should be kept a minimum from power lines:
   A. 5 ft (1.5m)
   B. 10 ft (3m)
   C. 15 ft (4.5m)
   D. 20 ft (6m)

Answer - B
Reference - FFS, p 366

Ladders

9. For which situation is the three-fire-fighter flat shoulder ladder carry best suited?
   A. There are overhead obstructions
   B. The ladder must be maneuvered around sharp corners
   C. The ladder must be carried over short obstacles
   D. The ladder will be raised in a narrow space

Answer - B
Reference - FFS, p 376

10. The rails of a trussed beam are separated by:
    A. Tie rods
    B. Truss blocks
    C. A-plates
    D. I-beams

Answer - B
Reference - FFS, p 358

11. Which term describes a power-operated ladder that is permanently mounted on a fire apparatus?
    A. Aerial
    B. Extension
    C. Snorkel
    D. Quint

Answer - A
Reference - FFS, p 359

12. Which type of ladder should be carried by more than one fire fighter?
    A. Extension
    B. Single
    C. Roof
    D. Attic

Answer - A
Reference - FFS, p 371

Chapter 13

13. How often should ground ladders be visually inspected?
   A. Monthly
   B. Quarterly
   C. Annually
   D. Biannually

Answer - A
Reference - FFS, p 363

14. A ladder is carried at arm's length in a(n) carry:
   A. Quick
   B. Suitcase
   C. Arm
   D. Grab

Answer - B
Reference - FFS, p 374

15. Overextension of the fly section of an extension ladder is prevented by:
   A. Stops
   B. Pawls
   C. Guides
   D. Locks

Answer - A
Reference - FFS, p 359

16. Which action is potentially hazardous while raising an extension ladder?
   A. Hoisting the halyard with the hands in the "thumbs up" position
   B. Placing a foot on a rung
   C. Anchoring the ladder with a foot against a rail
   D. Tying off the halyard on a bed-section rung

Answer - B
Reference - FFS, p 387

Ladders

17. What are butt spurs on a ladder?
    A. Mechanical locks that hold the fly section in place
    B. Devices to secure the ladder to a roof ridge
    C. Bumps and dents that occur on the foot pad as a result of use
    D. Spikes on the base that keep it from slipping

Answer - D
Reference - FFS, p 357

18. Portable ladders approved for fire service use can support up to _____.
    A. 300lb (135 kg)
    B. 450lb (205 kg)
    C. 600 lb (270 kg)
    D. 750lb (340 kg)

Answer - D
Reference - FFS, p 367

19. Which term describes the top or bottom section of a trussed beam?
    A. Dog
    B. Block
    C. Rung
    D. Rail

Answer - D
Reference - FFS, p 357

20. What are the two main structural components that run the entire length of a ladder?
    A. Flies
    B. Rungs
    C. Beams
    D. Truss blocks

Answer - C
Reference - FFS, p 357

Chapter 13

21. What should be done with the excess halyard once an extension ladder is placed and extended?
    A. Use it to form an anchor point
    B. Let it hang between the ladder and the building
    C. Wrap it around rungs of the ladder
    D. Use it to tie off the bed section

Answer - C
Reference - FFS, p 381

22. When should the building be used to anchor the butt during a ladder raise?
    A. For any single-fire-fighter ladder raise
    B. When laddering a building without eaves
    C. When sending a roof ladder aloft
    D. When a single fire fighter raises an extension ladder

Answer - D
Reference - FFS, p 381

23. On a three-fire-fighter ladder carry, how should the fire fighters align themselves?
    A. Two at the butt, one at the tip
    B. All three on the same side of the ladder
    C. Two on one side, one on the other
    D. Two at the tip, one at the butt

Answer - B
Reference - FFS, p 373

24. Which statement is correct about sliding your hands long the underside of the beams while climbing a ladder?
    A. This practice provides you with three continuous points of contact.
    B. This practice is appropriate only when both hands are free.
    C. This practice is less secure than grabbing the rungs in a hand-over-hand manner.
    D. This practice is practical only on ladders with I-beam construction.

Answer - A
Reference - FFS, p 391

Ladders

25. What is the maximum personnel load for a fire-service ladder?
    A. One fire fighter plus one victim
    B. Two fire fighters
    C. Two fire fighters plus one victim
    D. Three fire fighters

Answer - C
Reference - FFS, p 367

26. Where should the tip of a ladder be placed for rescue operations from a window?
    A. Immediately below the sill
    B. Into the opening about three rungs
    C. On either side of the window, halfway up the opening
    D. About 3 feet above the window

Answer - A
Reference - FFS, p 368

27. How often should ladder service testing be performed?
    A. Monthly
    B. Quarterly
    C. Semi-annually
    D. Annually

Answer - D
Reference - FFS, p 366

28. Poles used to stabilize long extension ladders are called:
    A. Stay poles
    B. Side poles
    C. Guy poles
    D. Extension poles

Answer - A
Reference - FFS, p 359

29. Which part of a ladder directly bears the weight of the person climbing it?
    A. Tie rod
    B. Truss block
    C. Spur
    D. Rung

Answer - D
Reference - FFS, p 357

30. What is the function of stops on an extension ladder?
    A. Prevent overextension
    B. Prevent collapse in the event of halyard failure
    C. Prevent the ladder from slipping on the ground
    D. Lock the extended fly sections in place

Answer - A
Reference - FFS, p 359

31. What is the term for keeping a ladder from slipping by applying one's weight to the underside of it?
    A. Securing
    B. Tying-in
    C. Anchoring
    D. Heeling

Answer - D
Reference - FFS, p 388

32. The purpose of the hooks of a roof ladder is to:
    A. Provide safe attachment points for fire fighters working on the ladder
    B. Grip the eaves of the roof to keep the ladder from slipping
    C. Prevent the butt of the ladder from slipping or shifting
    D. Secure the tip of the ladder to the peak of a pitched roof

Answer - D
Reference - FFS, p 358

33. Which part of the ladder is raised or extended from the bed section?
    A. Tip
    B. Fly
    C. Extension
    D. Guide

Answer - B
Reference - FFS, p 358

34. Which knot is used to tie off a ladder halyard?
    A. Clove hitch
    B. Sheepshank
    C. Figure eight
    D. Bowline on a bight

Answer - A
Reference - FFS, p 382

35. Which part(s) of a ladder should not be exposed to solvents?
    A. All parts
    B. Beams
    C. Halyard
    D. Pawls

Answer - C
Reference - FFS, p 364

36. What is the maximum reach for a 28-ft (8.5-m) ladder?
    A. The second story roof
    B. The second story windows with two rungs inside
    C. The second story windowsills only
    D. The third-story roof

Answer - A
Reference - FFS, p 369

Chapter 13

37. Which part of the ladder is placed against the ground when the ladder is raised?
    A. Butt
    B. Dog
    C. Heel
    D. Bed

Answer - A
Reference - FFS, p 357

38. What is the maximum length of a straight or roof ladder that can be carried safely by one fire fighter?
    A. 12 ft (3.65 m)
    B. 14 ft (4.25 m)
    C. 16 ft (5 m)
    D. 18 ft (5.5 m)

Answer - D
Reference - FFS, p 371

39. A ladder _____ is used to lower a rescuer into a trench or manhole.
    A. Frame
    B. Tripod
    C. Gin
    D. Anchor

Answer - C
Reference - FFS, p 357

40. In the one-fire-fighter carry, where is the top beam of the ladder?
    A. Above the head
    B. Under the arm
    C. On the shoulder
    D. In the hands

Answer - C
Reference - FFS, p 371

Notes on Ladders

Parts of a ladder
1. Beam - Main structural component on either side of the ladder. Trussed (top and bottom rails), I-beam (thick top and bottom sections with thinner middle section), and solid beam (common in wood ladders).
2. Rail - top or bottom section of a trussed beam
3. Truss block - piece that joins the two rails of a trussed beam
4. Rung - crosspiece that spans two beams of a ladder
5. Tie rod - metal bar that runs from one beam of a ladder to the other, preventing the beams from separating. Often found in wooden ladders.
6. Tip - top of the ladder
7. Butt - end of the ladder which is placed against the ground
8. Butt spurs - metal spikes attached to the butt of a ladder to prevent slipping
9. Butt plate - metal spike plus a cleat to prevent slipping.
10. Roof hooks - spring loaded, retractible, curved metal hooks to hold the tip of a ladder to the peak of a pitched roof.
11. Heat sensor label - indicates when a ladder has been exposed to excessive heat.
12. Protection plates - plates attached to a ladder at chafing or friction points.

Extension ladder
1. Bed (base) section -
2. Fly section - raised or extended part
3. Guides - strips of metal or wood to guide the fly section during extension
4. Halyard - rope or cable used to raise or lower the fly section
5. Pawls - mechanical locks that hold the ladder once it is extended.
6. Stops - pieces of wood or metal that prevent the fly section from being extended too far.
7. Staypole (tormentor) - long metal spike attached to the top of the bed section which stabilizes the ladder in extension.

Chapter 14
Search and Rescue

1. What is the correct procedure for vent—entry—search?
   A. Use this process in combination with horizontal ventilation
   B. Vent the window as soon as possible after entering the room
   C. Searchers must be equipped with a hose line
   D. Close the door as soon as possible after making entry

Answer - D
Reference - FFS, p 413

2. A quick attempt to locate potential victims who may be in danger is a(n) _____.
   A. Primary search
   B. Rapid sweep
   C. Initial survey
   D. Secondary search

Answer - A
Reference - FFS, p 407

3. During a fire, where is a missing child likely to be located?
   A. In his or her parent's bed
   B. In the kitchen
   C. Hiding in a closet
   D. In an exit pathway

Answer - C
Reference - FFS, p 408

4. Which statement about vent—entry—search is correct?
   A. Searchers enter and exit the search room through an interior door
   B. The process begins prior to fire attack
   C. The process puts the searcher between the fire and a ventilation opening
   D. Vent—entry—search is practical only for single-story buildings

Answer - C
Reference - FFS, p 413

Search and Rescue

5. How does the fire fighter move when performing the fire fighter drag?
   A. Crawling on hands and knees
   B. Walking forward
   C. Walking backward
   D. Duck-walking

Answer - A
Reference - FFS, p 424, 427

6. When lowering an unconscious child down a ladder, where should the rescuer's hands be?
   A. On the same rung
   B. On the beams
   C. On different rungs
   D. One on a rung, the other on a beam

Answer - B
Reference - FFS, p 434

7. During an unconscious-victim ladder rescue, what is the position of the victim?
   A. Upright, facing the rescuer
   B. Horizontal, facing the ladder
   C. Upright, facing the ladder
   D. Horizontal, facing the rescuer

Answer - A
Reference - FFS, p 431

8. When using a webbing sling drag, what helps support the victim's head and neck?
   A. The webbing sling
   B. The rescuer's hands
   C. The rescuer's forearms
   D. A roll of blanket

Answer - A
Reference - FFS, p 424

Chapter 14

9. The first priority for search teams is those areas:
   A. Where victims are most likely to be found
   B. With the highest number of occupants
   C. Where trapped occupants have the best chance for survival
   D. where occupants are in the most immediate danger

Answer - D
Reference - FFS, p 407

10. Adult fire victims are often found _____.
    A. Under a bed
    B. In a closet
    C. In a bathtub
    D. Near a door

Answer - D
Reference - FFS, p 408

11. How does vent—entry—search differ from conventional search and rescue?
    A. The fire is ventilated before entry is made
    B. A window is used for entry and exit
    C. The fire fighter is attached to a guide rope
    D. All windows and doors are propped open during the search

Answer - A
Reference - FFS, p 413

12. When organizing teams for a large building search, assignments are often based on:
    A. Known areas of safe refuge
    B. Alarm panel indicators
    C. Wind direction
    D. Stairway locations

Answer - D
Reference - FFS, p 407

13. What is the main purpose of the secondary search?
    A. Remove remaining occupants
    B. Locate deceased victims
    C. Double-check the primary search area
    D. Find evidence of cause and origin

Answer - B
Reference - FFS, p 408

14. Which piece of equipment should be used whenever possible during an emergency drag from a vehicle?
    A. Short backboard
    B. Webbing
    C. Long backboard
    D. Blanket

Answer - C
Reference - FFS, p 424

15. Which area is the first search priority?
    A. The area immediately around the fire
    B. Exit pathways
    C. The higher-level floors
    D. The rooms most likely to be occupied

Answer - A
Reference - FFS, p 407

16. A blanket drag is best suited for a victim who:
    A. Is not dressed
    B. May have a spinal injury
    C. Is grossly obese
    D. Is a child

Answer - A
Reference - FFS, p 421

Chapter 14

17. Which method of evacuation for victims above ground should be avoided whenever possible?
    A. Aerial device
    B. Ground ladder
    C. Fire escape
    D. Interior stairway

Answer - B
Reference - FFS, p 417

18. Which step should be performed before beginning search and rescue?
    A. Go directly to the most severely threatened area of the structure
    B. Perform a risk—benefit analysis
    C. Deploy a hose line or tagline
    D. Perform a primary survey

Answer - B
Reference - FFS, p 405

19. When is an exception made to the two-in/two-out rule?
    A. There are no exceptions; the rule applies to all IDLH entries
    B. When it will delay operations due to lack of personnel
    C. In life-threatening situations where immediate action can save a life
    D. In IDLH entries where there is no visible fire

Answer - A
Reference - FFS, p

20. Which means of victim removal should be avoided if possible?
    A. Fire escape
    B. Stairway
    C. Aerial tower
    D. Aerial ladder

Answer - D
Reference - FFS, p 417

21. The two-person chair carry is particularly useful _____.
    A. For victims with possible spinal injury
    B. In heavy smoke conditions
    C. For obese victims
    D. in narrow corridors

Answer - D
Reference - FFS, p 419

22. Where does the victim's arm go in the one-person walking assist?
    A. Around the rescuer's waist
    B. Linked in the rescuer's arm
    C. Around the rescuer's neck
    D. Across the victim's chest

Answer - C
Reference - FFS, p 418

23. When lives can be saved, how much risk is justified in trying to save them?
    A. Minimal
    B. Moderate
    C. High
    D. Unlimited

Answer - C
Reference - FFS, p 404, 415

24. What is the biggest drawback of the two-person seat carry?
    A. Rescuers must maintain a stooped posture
    B. It is difficult to travel long distances
    C. It is difficult to move through doors
    D. The carry requires access to a chair

Answer - C
Reference - FFS, p 418

Chapter 14

25. If you encounter a closed door during a search, what should you do before entering?
    A. Try before you pry
    B. Gap the door
    C. Loudly identify yourself and your intentions
    D. Check the door for heat

Answer - D
Reference - FFS, p

26. When rescuing a conscious person from a window using a ladder, where does the second fire fighter stand?
    A. On the bottom rung of the ladder
    B. About six rungs down from the top
    C. On a rung level with the opening
    D. One rung below the windowsill

Answer - D
Reference - FFS, p 430

27. Which statement best describes a primary search?
    A. A primary search is a quick search for victims in immediate danger.
    B. A primary search is a rapid initial assessment of life-threatening conditions.
    C. A primary search is an extensive and thorough search for potential victims.
    D. A primary search is a rapid search for victims after initial knockdown.

Answer - A
Reference - FFS, p 407

28. In which type of search pattern do fire fighters turn right upon entry to a room and then turn left at each corner around the room?
    A. Oriented
    B. Counterclockwise
    C. Left-hand
    D. Standard

Answer – B
Reference - FFS, p

150

Search and Rescue

29. What is the best source of information for identifying building layout, stairways, and exits?
   A. 360° survey
   B. Preincident plan
   C. Occupant description
   D. Initial entry crews

Answer - B
Reference - FFS, p 407

30. Weighing the potential danger to fire fighters against the potential for saving a life is called _____.
   A. Primary survey
   B. Life-safety analysis
   C. Triage
   D. Risk—benefit analysis

Answer - D
Reference - FFS, p 405

31. When vent—entry—search is performed with two fire fighters, where is the second fire fighter located?
   A. In constant physical contact with the first searcher
   B. At the anchor point
   C. Just outside the window
   D. The doorway

Answer - D
Reference - FFS, p 413

32. How much risk to fire fighters is acceptable in attempting to save valuable property?
   A. None
   B. Limited
   C. Significant
   D. Unlimited

Answer - B
Reference - FFS, p 415

151

33. Which carry works best for children and small adults?
    A. Chair
    B. Cradle-in-arms
    C. Extremities
    D. Incline

Answer - B
Reference - FFS, p 419

34. What is a critical factor to evaluate in size-up for search and rescue?
    A. Reflex time
    B. Type of fire attack
    C. Victims' ability to self-evacuate
    D. Age of victims

Answer - C
Reference - FFS, p 405

35. What is the correct procedure during a clockwise room search?
    A. The crew turns left at each corner
    B. The crew turns right at the entry point
    C. The left hand sweeps the middle of the room
    D. The left hand maintains contact with the wall

Answer – D
Reference - FFS, p

36. Where should a search rope be anchored?
    A. At the entry point
    B. To each rescuer
    C. To a hauling system
    D. To a second exit

Answer - A
Reference - FFS, p 413

Search and Rescue

37. What is the best way to confirm everyone has safely evacuated a building?
    A. Question occupants
    B. Conduct a head count
    C. Conduct a personnel accountability report
    D. Conduct a thorough search

Answer - D
Reference - FFS, p 404

38. Which emergency drag is best for fast removal from a dangerous area?
    A. Clothes
    B. Blanket
    C. Extremities
    D. Webbing sling

Answer - A
Reference - FFS, p 421

39. Which statement regarding the fire fighter drag is correct?
    A. It requires no equipment to carry out.
    B. It is well suited to stairways.
    C. It can be used when the victim is heavier than the rescuer.
    D. It requires cooperation on the part of the victim.

Answer - C
Reference - FFS, p 424

40. The one-person walking assist is best suited for victims who are:
    A. Awake and responsive
    B. Unable to walk
    C. Require support to walk
    D. Capable of walking

Answer - D
Reference - FFS, p 418

Chapter 14

41. Which statement is correct?
    A. Searching a building is completed in two different operations, primary and secondary search
    B. During the secondary search, the team is often ahead of attack lines and may be above the fire.
    C. The secondary search takes place in a rapid but thorough manner in areas most likely to have victims.
    D. The secondary search is the most dangerous.

Answer - A
Reference - FFS, p 407

42. Which items would be found in the risk/benefit philosophy of a risk management plan?
    A. Firefighting is inherently risky, so it is impossible to try to reduce risk through Standard Operating Guides/Standard Operating Procedures.
    B. Significant risk to the life of a firefighter shall be limited to those situations where the firefighter can potentially save endangered lives.
    C. Where no life or valued property can be saved, risk may be taken by firefighters.
    D. Firefighters should enter every abandoned structure heavily involved in fire as it may be occupied.

Answer - B
Reference - FFS, p 405

43. Successful fire attack on structures should be:
    A. Coordinated with other activities, such as ventilation and rescue.
    B. Coordinated with overhaul operations to protect contents on the fire floor. L/DH
    C. Deployed only when six or more firefighters are on scene.
    D. Only attempted by certified firefighters.

Answer - A
Reference - FFS, p 404

Notes on Search and Rescue

Primary search - quick search while the fire is ongoing to look for survivors
Secondary search - slower search done after the fire is out, typically during salvage and overhaul, looking for deceased victims.

Search priorities
1. Areas where victims may be located immediately around the fire.
2. Areas directly above the fire
3. Higher level floors, working from top floors down.
4. Areas below the fire floor.

Chapter 15
Ventilation

1. What is the sudden, explosive ignition of fire gases that occurs when oxygen is introduced into a superheated space?
   A. Mushrooming
   B. Rollover
   C. Flashover
   D. Backdraft

Answer - D
Reference - FFS, p 447

2. What are gusset plates?
   A. Long strips of metal that are sandwiched by wood beam members
   B. Truss-component connecting plates made of lightweight metal
   C. The vertical members of a truss assembly
   D. Structural sheathing designed to resist shear forces

Answer - B
Reference - FFS, p 465

3. All forms of ventilation that use fans or other powered equipment are classified as _____ ventilation:
   A. Assisted
   B. Hydraulic
   C. Mechanical
   D. Positive pressure

Answer - C
Reference - FFS, p 449

4. What is the greatest danger to fire fighters performing vertical ventilation?
   A. Roof collapse
   B. Smoke and heat release through the vent hole
   C. Fire lapping up from under an eave
   D. Falling off the roof or ladder

Answer - A
Reference - FFS, p 464

Ventilation

5. Which type of ventilation opening is used to stop fire spread in a long, narrow building?
   A. Peak
   B. Louvered
   C. Triangular
   D. Trench

Answer - D
Reference - FFS, p 474

6. Which structural component is composed of relatively small and lightweight components arranged in a series of triangles?
   A. Joist
   B. Truss
   C. Lintel
   D. Chord

Answer - B
Reference - FFS, p 465

7. Which fuel produces large quantities of black, roiling smoke that rises in a vertical column?
   A. Vegetation
   B. Wood
   C. Petroleum products
   D. Textiles

Answer - C
Reference - FFS, p

8. What is the phenomenon in which smoke hangs low to the ground on a calm, cool, damp day?
   A. Ground effect
   B. Pooling
   C. Down drafting
   D. Smoke inversion

Answer - D
Reference - FFS, p 451

Chapter 15

9. How do thermopane windows affect fire behavior?
   A. Decrease the likelihood of backdraft
   B. Improve ventilation
   C. Allow for faster heat build-up within the structure
   D. Are more likely to break when exposed to heat

Answer - C
Reference - FFS, p 449

10. Positive-pressure ventilation is the least suitable approach for which situation?
    A. Fire attack is in progress
    B. Structure with large interior spaces
    C. Fire in structural void spaces
    D. High-rise fire

Answer - C
Reference - FFS, p

11. What must be done before beginning ventilation?
    A. The main body of the fire must be knocked down
    B. The primary search must be complete
    C. The hose team must be in place and ready to attack the fire
    D. The rapid intervention crew must be assigned and ready

Answer - C
Reference - FFS, p 445

12. Which type of roof opening extends all the way across the roof from one exterior wall to the other?
    A. Band
    B. Trench
    C. Transverse
    D. Cross

Answer - B
Reference - FFS, p 474

Ventilation

13. What is the term for the weather-resistant surface of a roof?
    A. Decking
    B. Covering
    C. Skin
    D. Tar paper

Answer - B
Reference - FFS, p 464

14. Which statement about the operation of HVAC equipment during fire ventilation operations is correct?
    A. HVAC systems are designed to automatically shut down when smoke is detected.
    B. Some HVAC systems incorporate features that are useful for clearing smoke.
    C. It is important to maintain power to the HVAC system at all times.
    D. HVAC systems should be shut down as soon as possible.

Answer - B
Reference - FFS, p 457

15. What is the term for the process in which heated products of combustion spread outward and downward?
    A. Mushrooming
    B. Stack effect
    C. Stratification
    D. Thermal imbalance

Answer - A
Reference - FFS, p

16. What are smoke, heat, and toxic gases called collectively?
    A. Fire gases
    B. Black fire
    C. Smoke
    D. Products of combustion

Answer - D
Reference - FFS, p 452

159

17. Which form of ventilation is best for potential backdraft conditions?
    A. Positive pressure
    B. Horizontal
    C. Negative pressure
    D. Vertical

Answer - D
Reference - FFS, p 447

18. Which type of building is the most prone to the stack effect?
    A. Warehouse
    B. Cold-storage facility
    C. High-rise
    D. Shopping mall

Answer - C
Reference - FFS, p 477

19. Which statement summarizes the overall effect of negative-pressure ventilation?
    A. It pulls smoke out.
    B. It displaces the contaminated atmosphere.
    C. It pushes smoke out.
    D. It releases the contaminated atmosphere.

Answer - A
Reference - FFS, p 449

20. What is sounding?
    A. Checking the condition of a roof by striking it with a tool
    B. Probing a closet or confined space with a tool handle
    C. Using a screwdriver or similar tool to check the depth of char
    D. Listening for fire inside concealed spaces

Answer - A
Reference - FFS, p 463

21. When making louver cuts, what is used as a fulcrum to make the louvered openings?
    A. Ridge pole
    B. Decking
    C. Roof support
    D. Purlin

Answer - C
Reference - FFS, p 472

22. How do heated gases move in a room?
    A. They disperse evenly throughout the entire volume of the room
    B. They rise to the ceiling and spread outward
    C. They spread laterally to the walls and then begin to rise
    D. They seek the lowest point and settle there

Answer - B
Reference - FFS, p 452

23. What does fast-moving smoke indicate?
    A. Poorly ventilated fire
    B. Extremely hot fire
    C. High synthetic fuel content
    D. Incomplete combustion

Answer - B
Reference - FFS, p 451

24. Which type of ventilation relies on doors and windows on the same level as the fire?
    A. Positive pressure
    B. Passive
    C. Horizontal
    D. Natural

Answer - C
Reference - FFS, p 451

Chapter 15

25. When ventilating the basement, where is the preferred location to ventilate?
    A. The most accessible location
    B. The point farthest away from the entrance used by the fire attack crew
    C. The stairway from the upper level
    D. Any preexisting opening

Answer - D
Reference - FFS, p 476

26. For natural ventilation, which windows should be opened last?
    A. Those windows in rooms not directly involved in fire
    B. Those windows opening directly into the fire room
    C. Leeward windows
    D. Upwind windows

Answer - D
Reference - FFS, p 452

27. What is correct procedure when cutting a ventilation opening in a roof?
    A. Several small holes distributed over the fire are better than one large hole
    B. Use preexisting openings only when there is no alternative
    C. Rock the saw over, rather than through, structural supports
    D. Return the saw to idle before withdrawing it from a cut

Answer - C
Reference - FFS, p

28. In ordinary construction, exterior walls are made of
    A. Noncombustible or limited-combustible materials
    B. Any standard load-bearing material
    C. Fire-resistive materials
    D. Combustible materials

Answer - A
Reference - FFS, p 449

Ventilation

29. What is the term for cool, stagnant interior smoke?
   A. Layering
   B. Stratification
   C. Stacking
   D. Inversion

Answer - D
Reference - FFS, p 451

30. A problem with using doorways as ventilation openings is that:
   A. The large opening can admit too much air
   B. This technique tends to produce churning
   C. It is more difficult to control the ventilation process
   D. This technique compromises personnel entry and exit

Answer - D
Reference - FFS, p 443,444

31. Churning most frequently occurs with which form of ventilation?
   A. Positive pressure
   B. Vertical
   C. Horizontal
   D. Negative pressure

Answer - D
Reference - FFS, p 458

32. Which hazard is of particular concern in a basement fire?
   A. Smoke and heat venting up the stairs toward fire fighters
   B. An air-tight compartment prone to backdraft
   C. Storage of flammable/hazardous materials
   D. Excessive property damage from cutting interior vent holes

Answer - A
Reference - FFS, p 476

33. What occurs when room temperature reaches the ignition point of the combustibles within it?
    A. Mushrooming
    B. Backdraft
    C. Flashover
    D. Lapping

Answer - C
Reference - FFS, p 447

34. How can churning be eliminated during smoke ejection?
    A. Pull the fan back a few inches
    B. Completely block the opening around the fan
    C. Increase the number or size of exhaust openings
    D. Raise the fan in the opening

Answer - D
Reference - FFS, p 458

35. What is the term for the main area of the fire?
    A. Origin
    B. Body
    C. Heel
    D. Seat

Answer - D
Reference - FFS, p 461

36. Which type of ventilation uses openings in roofs or floors so that heat and smoke can escape the structure in an upward direction?
    A. Horizontal
    B. Mechanical
    C. Vertical
    D. Negative pressure

Answer - C
Reference - FFS, p 451

Ventilation

37. What is the term for the transfer of heat through a circulating medium of liquid or gas?
   A. Conduction
   B. Radiation
   C. Condensation
   D. Convection

Answer - D
Reference - FFS, p 452

38. Smoke produced by a small fire involving ordinary combustibles is:
   A. Gray and fast moving
   B. Black and thick
   C. Mustard or brown and wispy
   D. Light colored and lazy

Answer - D
Reference - FFS, p

39. Lightweight trusses are typically used in which roof type(s)?
   A. Arched
   B. Pitched
   C. Flat
   D. Many types

Answer - D
Reference - FFS, p 465

40. Which item is used in negative-pressure ventilation?
   A. Smoke ejector
   B. Blower
   C. HVAC system
   D. Negative-pressure fan

Answer - A
Reference - FFS, p 457

Chapter 15

41. Which benefit is most likely to result from properly performed ventilation?
    A. Reduced fire intensity
    B. Improved conditions within the structure
    C. Prevention of fire extension to uninvolved areas
    D. Protection of exterior exposures

Answer - B
Reference - FFS, p 442, 450

42. What is the minimum measurement for a ventilation opening cut in a roof?
    A. 4 ft by 4 ft (1.2 m by 1.2 m)
    B. 5 ft by 5 ft (1.5 m by 1.5 m)
    C. 6 ft by 6 ft (1.8 m by 1.8 m)
    D. 6 ft by 8ft (1.8 m by 2.4 m)

Answer - A
Reference - FFS, p 469

43. Which term means the spread of fire from one floor to another via exterior windows?
    A. Laddering
    B. Leap frogging
    C. Stack effect
    D. Crowning

Answer - B
Reference - FFS, p

44. A freestanding wall that extends above the roofline is a _____ wall.
    A. Parapet
    B. Pony
    C. Curtain
    D. Sleeper

Answer - A
Reference - FFS, p 466

Ventilation

45. What is a characteristic of bowstring trusses?
    A. Lack of a cockloft or storage space
    B. Commonly used in lightweight residential construction
    C. Commonly used in fire-resistive construction
    D. Prone to sudden collapse in fire conditions

Answer - D
Reference - FFS, p 468

Notes on Ventilation

Reason
1. Gives occupants a greater chance of survival
2. Makes searches faster
3. Prevents fire spread
4. Fire attacks get easier because of allowing steam to leave and better visibility
5. Reduce property damage by reducing damage from smoke, heat, and water.

Indications of roof collapse
1. Visible sagging
2. Roof separating from walls
3. Structural failure in another part of building
4. Sudden increase in fire intensity
5. High heat indicators and thermal imaging camera

Consider how much water you are putting into the building. Water weight can collapse floors

Chapter 16
Water Supply

1. What is used to carry a self-locking twin-doughnut hose roll?
    A. Webbing
    B. A loop of hose
    C. Hose strap
    D. Rope

Answer - B
Reference - FFS, p 522

2. The pipes that deliver water to users and hydrants on individual streets are:
    A. Service lines
    B. Secondaries
    C. Distributors
    D. Cross mains

Answer - C
Reference - FFS, p 494

3. What is the correct tool to tighten a hard-suction hose connection?
    A. Rubber mallet
    B. Spanner
    C. Hose wrench
    D. Strap wrench

Answer - A
Reference - FFS, p 512

4. Pressure in a water distribution system during average consumption is _____.
    A. Residual
    B. Mean
    C. Normal operating
    D. Static

Answer - C
Reference - FFS, p 501

Water Supply

5. The pressure remaining in a water distribution system when water is flowing is the _____ pressure.
   A. Static
   B. Operating
   C. Flow
   D. Residual

Answer – D
Reference - FFS, p 501

6. A typical number fire engine carries _____ of supply hose.
   A. 500 to 750 ft (150 to 228 m)
   B. 750 to 1250 ft (228 to 380 m)
   C. 1000 to 1500 ft (305 to 457 m)
   D. 1500 to 2000 ft (457 to 610 m)

Answer – B
Reference - FFS, p 511

7. What is the function of lugs found on couplings?
   A. Align the threads during coupling
   B. Aid in coupling and uncoupling hose
   C. Help the coupling slide over obstructions
   D. Strengthen the coupling

Answer - B
Reference - FFS, p 506

8. Couplings are tightened and loosened with a _____ wrench.
   A. Hydrant
   B. Lug
   C. Hose
   D. Spanner

Answer - D
Reference - FFS, p 506

9. What makes a water thief different from a wye is the addition of _____.
   A. A second inlet
   B. Ball valves
   C. A 2 ½ (65-mm) outlet
   D. Clapper valves

Answer - C
Reference - FFS, p 515

10. The NFPA recommends color-coding hydrants to indicate _____.
    A. The most recent flow test
    B. Available pressure
    C. The water source
    D. Available flow

Answer - D
Reference - FFS, p 498

11. Which of the following is required to be noted on the hose record?
    A. Test duration
    B. Test date
    C. Test pressure
    D. Date of last use

Answer - B
Reference - FFS, p 515

12. What is the color code for a hydrant flowing 1500 gpm (5678 lpm) or more?
    A. White
    B. Orange
    C. Green
    D. Light blue

Answer - D
Reference - FFS, p 499

Water Supply

13. In a _____ lay, the hose is laid out from the fire to the hydrant.
   A. Relay
   B. Defensive
   C. Rreverse
   D. Hydrant

Answer - C
Reference - FFS, p 511

14. What is the realistic minimum usable residual pressure from a water distribution system for firefighting operations?
   A. 0 psi (0 kPa)
   B. 20 psi (138 kPa)
   C. 30 psi (207 kPa)
   D. 40 psi (276kPa)

Answer - B
Reference - FFS, p 501

15. Which type of hose coupling does not have male or female ends?
   A. Ramos
   B. Snap-tite
   C. Storz
   D. Naval

Answer - C
Reference - FFS, p 507

16. In general, mobile water supply apparatus carry _____.
   A. 1000 or fewer gal (3785 L or fewer)
   B. 1000 to 3500 gal (3785t0 13,249 L)
   C. 2000 to 5000 gal (7570 to 18,927 L)
   D. 3000 to 6000 gal (11,356 22,712 L)

Answer - B
Reference - FFS, p 490

17. How close must a fire engine get to a static water source to be able to draft directly from it through hard suction hose?
    A. A distance equal to the total length of the available hard suction hose minus 10 ft
    B. 10 ft (3m)
    C. 20 ft (6m)
    D. 30 ft (9m)

Answer - C
Reference - FFS, p 489

18. Fire fighters may need to hold on to the _____ while filling a self-expanding portable tank.
    A. Frame
    B. Hose
    C. Rope
    D. Collar

Answer - D
Reference - FFS, p 491

19. Which supply line load is capable of laying both single and dual supply lines?
    A. Twin
    B. Detroit
    C. Horseshoe
    D. Split bed

Answer - D
Reference - FFS, p 529

20. What is the term for the large discharge opening on a fire hydrant?
    A. Steamer
    B. Deluge
    C. Main
    D. Primary

Answer - A
Reference - FFS, p 499

Water Supply

21. What is a function of a hose liner?
    A. Withstand water pressure
    B. Resist mechanical damage
    C. Reduce friction loss
    D. Protect against thermal damage

Answer - C
Reference - FFS, p 505

22. What is used to connect individual sections of hose together to extend their length?
    A. Appliance
    B. Coupling
    C. Higbee
    D. Rocker

Answer - B
Reference - FFS, p 505

23. Which tool is used to protect a hose line that is being hoisted over a sharp edge?
    A. Hose ramp
    B. Edge protector
    C. Hose pulley
    D. Hose roller

Answer - D
Reference - FFS, p 517

24. Hose that is at least 3½" (88 mm) in diameter is considered _____ diameter.
    A. Small
    B. Medium
    C. Large
    D. Master

Answer - C
Reference - FFS, p 505

Chapter 16

25. During annual testing, attack hose is tested at what pressure?
    A. 200 psi (1379 kPa)
    B. 300 psi (2068 kPa)
    C. 400 psi (2757 kPa)
    D. 500 psi (3447 kPa)

Answer - B
Reference - FFS, p 505

26. The two-fire-fighter stiff-arm method is used to _____.
    A. Advance a charged line
    B. Uncouple hose
    C. Reload LDH into a hose bed
    D. Make hard suction hose connections

Answer - B
Reference - FFS, p 510

27. Which pressure must be measured to calculate the quantity of water flowing through a hydrant discharge?
    A. Head
    B. Operating
    C. Flow
    D. Residual

Answer - C
Reference - FFS, p 501

28. What is the last step in rolling a straight hose roll?
    A. Connect the couplings together
    B. Use a foot to align protruding hose
    C. Create a fold to protect the outer coupling
    D. Tie the slip knot

Answer - B
Reference - FFS, p 519

Water Supply

29. Which device splits one hose stream into two hose streams?
   A. Siamese
   B. Splitter
   C. Wye
   D. Water thief

Answer - C
Reference - FFS, p 515

30. The pipes that deliver water from the treatment facility for distribution are _____.
   A. Secondaries
   B. Mains
   C. Distributors
   D. Trunks

Answer - B
Reference - FFS, p 492

31. Where are dry-barrel hydrants typically used?
   A. Static water supplies
   B. Cold climates
   C. Dedicated fire protection water systems
   D. Areas subject to frequent vandalism

Answer - B
Reference - FFS, p 495

32. How does a doughnut hose roll differ from a straight hose roll?
   A. Both couplings are in the middle
   B. The two couplings are connected
   C. Both couplings are on the outside
   D. The female coupling is on the outside

Answer - C
Reference - FFS, p 518

Chapter 16

33. Portable pumps can deliver a maximum of:
   A. 250 gpm (946 lpm)
   B. 500 gpm (1893 lpm)
   C. 750 gpm (2839 lpm)
   D. 1000 gpm (3785 lpm)

Answer - B
Reference - FFS, p 489

34. In a jacketed fire hose, which function does the outer jacket serve?
   A. It adds strength that allows the hose to withstand water pressure
   B. It is the waterproof layer of the hose
   C. It reduces friction loss
   D. It resists kinking

Answer - D
Reference - FFS, p 505

35. A Pitot gauge is used to determine _____ pressure.
   A. Static
   B. Residual
   C. Operating
   D. Flow

Answer - D
Reference - FFS, p 501

36. According to the NFPA, what is the minimum distance between the center of a fire hydrant outlet and the finished grade of the ground around the hydrant?
   A. 12" (30 cm)
   B. 18" (45 cm)
   C. 24" (60 cm)
   D. 30" (75 cm)

Answer - B
Reference - FFS, p 499

Water Supply

37. What is the color code for a hydrant flowing less than 500 gpm (1890 lpm)?
   A. Red
   B. Orange
   C. Yellow
   D. White

Answer - A
Reference - FFS, p 499

38. Which type of adaptor is used to connect two female couplings to each other?
   A. Wye
   B. Double female
   C. Siamese
   D. Double male

Answer - D
Reference - FFS, p 516

39. Which NFPA standard covers fire hose?
   A. 1962
   B. 1972
   C. 1982
   D. 1992

Answer - A
Reference - FFS, p 512

40. An engine lays hose from a water source to the fire scene in a _____ lay.
   A. Single
   B. Standard
   C. Basic
   D. Forward

Answer - D
Reference - FFS, p 523

Chapter 16

41. Which type of hose roll is used to store hose on a storage rack?
    A. Straight
    B. Doughnut
    C. Twin
    D. Flat

Answer - A
Reference - FFS, p 518

42. The flow or quantity of water moving is measured in:
    A. Joules
    B. Cubic feet per minute (cubic meters per minute)
    C. Gallons per minute (liters per minute)
    D. Pounds per square inch (kilopascals)

Answer - C
Reference - FFS, p 500

43. What should be done to avoid water hammer?
    A. Always maintain a minimum residual pressure of 20 psi
    B. Never connect a hard-suction hose to a pressurized water supply
    C. Purge air from the line before opening a valve or nozzle
    D. Open and close all valves slowly

Answer - D
Reference - FFS, p 504

44. The end of the hose bed closest to the apparatus cab is the _____.
    A. Front
    B. Bulkhead
    C. Partition
    D. Back

Answer - A
Reference - FFS, p 531

Water Supply

45. Which coupling goes on the inside of a straight hose roll?
   A. Female
   B. Male
   C. Either
   D. Both couplings are attached

Answer - B
Reference - FFS, p 518

46. How can you determine that a dry-barrel hydrant is still draining?
   A. Place a hand on the stem nut and feel for vibration
   B. Look for a continuing trickle from the discharge outlet
   C. Place a hand over an outlet and feel for suction
   D. Listen carefully for a hissing sound

Answer - C
Reference - FFS, p 497

47. Which of the following is one of the three factors that determine friction loss?
   A. Ambient temperature
   B. Hose diameter
   C. Atmospheric pressure
   D. Water source

Answer – B
Reference - FFS, p 504

48. When charging a supply line at a hydrant, the fire fighter should
   A. Place the hose clamp before opening the hydrant
   B. Avoid standing between the hose line and the hydrant
   C. Check that the hydrant strap is secure
   D. Fully open the stem and then back it off one full turn

Answer - B
Reference - FFS, p 534

Chapter 16

49. The most likely cause of leaking between two joined couplings is a damaged or missing _____.
    A. Compression gasket
    B. Swivel gasket
    C. Shank gasket
    D. Expansion ring

Answer B
Reference - FFS, p 507

50. What is the color code for a hydrant flowing 500 to 999 gpm (1890 to 3780 lpm)?
    A. Red
    B. Orange
    C. Green
    D. Light blue

Answer B
Reference - FFS, p 499

51. A dry hydrant provides access to a _____.
    A. Minicipal water system
    B. Static water source
    C. Portable water tank
    D. Cistern or well

Answer B
Reference - FFS, p. 489

52. What is the maximum capacity of typical portable water tanks?
    A. 1500 gal (5678 L)
    B. 2000 gal (7570 L)
    C. 3500 gal (13249 L)
    D. 5000 gal (18927 L)

Answer D
Reference - FFS, p. 490

Water Supply

53. Which hose load has the hose up on its edge and laid side-to-side in the hose bed?
   A. Edge
   B. Fan-fold
   C. Combination
   D. Accordion

Answer - D
Reference - FFS, p 534

54. What is a common use for a hose clamp?
   A. Allow a hydrant tob be opened before the supply line is connected to the pump intake
   B. Control a burst section of hose line without interrupting water flow
   C. Allow for a quick-connect of an attack line to a pumper when the threads do not match
   D. Regulate pressure/volume in a single hose

Answer B
Reference - FFS, p. 517

55. Which pipe pattern supplies water to hydrants from more than one direction?
   A. Grid
   B. Engineered
   C. Duplex
   D. Parallel

Answer A
Reference - FFS, p. 494

56. Which valve is opened or closed by rotating a handle a quarter turn?
   A. Gate
   B. Siamese
   C. Butterfly
   D. Slide

Answer C
Reference - FFS, p. 517

57. Which hose load has the hose up on its edge and placed around the perimeter of the hose bed in a U shape?
   A. Split
   B. U
   C. Horseshoe
   D. Perimeter

Answer C
Reference - FFS, p. 531

58. What is the fastest way for a mobile water supply apparatus to offload water into a portable tank?
   A. Connect to the drafting pumper
   B. Use the dump valve
   C. Engage the tender's auxiliary pump
   D. Use large-diameter hose

Answer B
Reference - FFS, p. 490

59. What is the maximum length of the conneected hose during hose testing?
   A. 300 ft (91 m)
   B. 400 ft (122 m)
   C. 500 ft (152 m)
   D. 600 ft (183 m)

Answer A
Reference - FFS, p.

60. The volume of water that is being moved through a pipe or hose is termed the _____.
   A. Pressure
   B. Flow
   C. Throughput
   D. Stream

Answer B
Reference - FFS, p. 501

Water Supply

61. What should be used to clean fire hoses?
    A. Dilute bleach solution
    B. Mild detergent
    C. TSP (trisodium phosphate)
    D. Class A foam

Answer B
Reference - FFS, p. 513

62. When should the fire fighter at the hydrant charge the supply line?
    A. As soon as it is connected to the hydrant
    B. Upon receiving a signal from the driver/operator
    C. After the supply line is connected to the pump intake
    D. After placing the hose clamp

Answer B
Reference - FFS, p. 498

63. What is the purpose of the Higbee indicators?
    A. Make hose coupling easier and faster
    B. Indicate when the hose may be pulling out of the coupling
    C. Help disoriented fire fighters find their way out of a building
    D. Identify the thread standard type

Answer A
Reference - FFS, p. 507

64. A soft suction hose is used to connect a pumper to a _____.
    A. Standpipe/FDC
    B. Master stream device
    C. Static water supply
    D. Hydrant

Answer D
Reference - FFS, p. 511

Chapter 16

65. Which feature of hose couplings is used to aid in the coupling and uncoupling of hose?
   A. Lug
   B. Shank
   C. Higbee cut
   D. Spanner

Answer A
Reference - FFS, p. 507

66. When filling a hoseline with water for testing, a pump pressure of approximately _____ psi is maintained.
   A. 250
   B. 25-30
   C. 50
   D. 80-90

Answer C
Reference - FFS, p.

67. According to the National Fire Protection Association (NFPA), a hydrant with an orange bonnet or caps may be expected to flow _____ gallons per minute.
   A. 500 to 999
   B. 1000 to 1499
   C. Greater than 1500
   D. Less than 500

Answer A
Reference - FFS, p. 499

Notes on Water Supply

Causes of hose damage
   1. Mechanical - glass damage from car and structure fires
   2. Heat and cold - destruction from flames
   3. Chemicals - HAZMAT incidents
   4. Mildew - storing hoses wet.

Change cross lays on an engine on a regular basis

Hose inspection
1. Test annually
2. Visual hose inspection quarterly
3. Keep hose records (a written history of each hose)

Chapter 17
Fire Attack and Foam

1. In general, what volume does a 2 ½" (64-mm) handline flow?
   A. 175 gpm (662 lpm)
   B. 200 gpm (757 lpm)
   C. 250 gpm (946 lpm)
   D. 300 gpm (1135 lpm)

Answer - C
Reference - FFS, p 553

2. Adding foam concentrate to a fire apparatus tank is called _____.
   A. Premixing
   B. Batch mixing
   C. Tank mixing
   D. Bulk mixing

Answer - B
Reference - FFS, p 576

3. What is the correct procedure for the triple-layer load?
   A. Half the load is shouldered, and the other half pays off from the ground
   B. The nozzle is attached to the bottom layer
   C. The entire load must be on the ground before the nozzle can be advanced
   D. Each layer should be a single length of hose

Answer - D
Reference - FFS, p 558

4. Which foam application method is best for a pool of flammable liquid on open ground?
   A. Bankshot (bank-down)
   B. Rain-down
   C. Sweep (roll-on)
   D. Subsurface injection

Answer - C
Reference - FFS, p 577

Fire Attack and Foam

5. What is a benefit of Class A foam?
    A. Does not conduct electricity
    B. Forms a vapor barrier on fuel spills
    C. Is compatible with many other foam types
    D. Reduces the surface tension of water

Answer - D
Reference - FFS, p 573

6. Which attack line load is often coupled to a larger-diameter line?
    A. Triple layer
    B. Split
    C. Minuteman
    D. Wyed lines

Answer - D
Reference - FFS, p 559

7. A 50' (15 m) section of charged 2 ½" (64 mm) hose weighs approximately _____?
    A. 100 lb. (45 kg)
    B. 125 lb. (57 kg)
    C. 150 lb. (68 kg)
    D. 200 lb. (91 kg)

Answer - C
Reference - FFS, p 553

8. Which foam application method is best for an open-top storage tank fire?
    A. Bankshot (bank-down)
    B. Rain-down
    C. Sweep (roll-on)
    D. Subsurface injection

Answer - A
Reference - FFS, p 577

Chapter 17

9. 1 ½" (38-mm) attack hose can flow _____.
   A. 50 to 100 gpm (189 to 379 lpm)
   B. 60 to 125 gpm (227 to 473 lpm)
   C. 75 to 150 gpm (284 to 566 lpm)
   D. 120 to 180 gpm (454 to 681 lpm)

Answer - B
Reference - FFS, p 553

10. Which preconnected hose load forms an S-shape in the hose bed?
    A. Triple layer
    B. Split
    C. Minuteman
    D. Skid

Answer - A
Reference - FFS, p 558

11. What is high-expansion foam particularly used for?
    A. Unignited fuel spills
    B. Exposure protection
    C. Transportation accidents
    D. Flooding of large enclosed areas

Answer - D
Reference - FFS, p 576

12. Which type of foam is particularly well suited for gasoline spills?
    A. Protein
    B. Fluoroprotein
    C. Aqueous film-forming
    D. Alcohol-resistant

Answer - C
Reference - FFS, p 575

13. To batch mix 3 percent foam into a 500-gallon (1893-liter) water tank, how much foam concentrate should be added to the tank?
    A. 3 gal (11.35 L)
    B. 5 gal (19 L)
    C. 9 gal (34 L)
    D. 15 gal (57 L)

Answer - D
Reference - FFS, p 576

14. What is the term for a hose line that is stored on an engine connected to a discharge and equipped with a nozzle for immediate deployment?
    A. Skid load
    B. Ready load
    C. Bundle
    D. Preconnect

Answer D
Reference – FFS, p 553

15. The low surface tension of Class A foam affects its extinguishing properties by _____.
    A. Raising the vaporization temperature of water
    B. Suppressing vapor production
    C. Diluting the fuel
    D. Enabling water to penetrate the fuel more deeply

Answer - D
Reference - FFS, p 573

16. Which type of nozzle is used most commonly with fluoroprotein foam?
    A. Fog
    B. Water aspirating
    C. Aerating
    D. Solid bore

Answer - C
Reference - FFS, p 576

Chapter 17

17. What is the second stage of advancing an attack line?
    A. Pulling the line from the bed
    B. Advancing the line to the point of attack
    C. Purging the line of air
    D. Flaking out the line at the building entrance

Answer - D
Reference - FFS, p 559

18. Which type of hose ranges in size from 1" to 1 ½" (25 to 38 mm) in diameter?
    A. Forestry
    B. Medium
    C. Handline
    D. Booster

Answer - A
Reference - FFS, p 553

19. Which type of load is most commonly used for preconnected attack lines?
    A. Minuteman
    B. Accordion
    C. Horseshoe
    D. Skid

Answer - A
Reference - FFS, p 554

20. When using a standpipe connection in a stairwell, how should the hose be arranged?
    A. Up the stairwell toward the floor above the fire
    B. Back and forth on the landing
    C. Down the stairwell toward the floor below the fire floor
    D. In large coils on the landing nearest the fire floor

Answer - A
Reference - FFS, p 567

Fire Attack and Foam

21. The function of a standpipe system is to provide _____.
    A. An auxiliary water supply for the fire department
    B. A connection from an engine to a static water source
    C. A connection for pumper support of a sprinkler system
    D. A water supply for interior attack lines

Answer - D
Reference - FFS, p 567

22. Which hose diameter is used as both supply line and attack handline?
    A. 1 ¾" (45 mm)
    B. 2 ½" (64 mm)
    C. 2 ¾" (70 mm)
    D. 3" (76mm)

Answer - B
Reference - FFS, p 552

23. Most smooth-bore nozzles are designed to operate at which pressure?
    A. 50 psi (345 kPa)
    B. 75 psi (517 kPa)
    C. 100 psi (690 kPa)
    D. 125 psi (862 kPa)

Answer - A
Reference - FFS, p 569

24. How does foam extinguish flammable liquid fires?
    A. Inhibits the chemical chain reaction
    B. Separates the fuel from the fire
    C. Dilutes the fuel
    D. Cools the fire

Answer - B
Reference - FFS, p 574

Chapter 17

25. What is an appropriate use for a 1" (25-mm) booster line?
    A. Exposure protection
    B. Car fire
    C. Appliance fire
    D. Dumpster fire

Answer - D
Reference - FFS, p 553

26. Attack lines should be connected to a standpipe system:
    A. One floor below the fire floor
    B. Two floors below the fire floor
    C. On the fire floor
    D. One floor above the fire floor

Answer - A
Reference - FFS, p 567

27. Which device mixes foam concentrate in the water stream in the proper percentage?
    A. Proportioner
    B. Mixer
    C. Aerator
    D. Aspirator

Answer - A
Reference - FFS, p 576

28. Which type of foam contains a surface-active agent that produces a fast-spreading film?
    A. High expansion
    B. Fluoroprotein
    C. Aqueous film-forming
    D. Class A

Answer - B
Reference - FFS, p 575

Fire Attack and Foam

29. When there is extra hose at the entry of a building, how should that hose be arranged?
    A. Large, loose coils
    B. A serpentine pattern
    C. A straight line
    D. Similar to an accordion fold

Answer - B
Reference - FFS, p 559

30. Most fog nozzles are designed to operate at which nozzle pressure?
    A. 50 psi (200 kPa)
    B. 75 psi (515kPa)
    C. 80 psi (550 kPa)
    D. 100 psi (690kPa)

Answer - D
Reference - FFS, p 570

31. Which attack line load is particularly useful when there is a long distance between the engine and the fire?
    A. Triple layer
    B. Wyed lines
    C. Minuteman
    D. Skid

Answer - B
Reference - FFS, p 559

32. Which nozzle type has the highest flow rate?
    A. Adjustable
    B. Handline
    C. Master stream
    D. Smooth bore

Answer - C
Reference - FFS, p 569

Chapter 17

33. What is the correct procedure for a burst hose line?
   A. Use two lengths of hose to replace a single burst length
   B. Leave the burst section in operation unless the water loss is affecting nozzle flow
   C. Place the clamp as far from the burst section of hose as possible
   D. Shut the line down at the pump panel only as last resort

Answer - A
Reference - FFS, p 568

34. Which type of foam is effective on polar solvents?
   A. Class A
   B. Fluoroprotein
   C. Aqueous film-forming
   D. Alcohol-resistant

Answer - D
Reference - FFS, p 574

35. What is the correct operating pressure for an in-line foam educator?
   A. 100 psi (689 kPa)
   B. 150 psi (1034 kPa)
   C. 200 psi (1379 kPa)
   D. 250 psi (1724 kPa)

Answer - C
Reference - FFS, p 576

36. Master streams flow a minimum of:
   A. 350 gpm (1335 lpm)
   B. 400 gpm (1514 lpm)
   C. 450 gpm (1703 lpm)
   D. 500 gpm (1893 lpm)

Answer - A
Reference - FFS, p 552

37. Which attack line load is particularly useful when the line must be advanced up a stairway?
    A. Triple layer
    B. Wyed lines
    C. Minuteman
    D. Skid

Answer - C
Reference - FFS, p 563

38. A 1-inch (45 mm) attack hose can flow:
    A. 60 to 125 gpm (227 to 473 lpm)
    B. 75 to 150 gpm (284 to 566 lpm)
    C. 100 to 160 gpm (379 to 606 lpm)
    D. 120 to 180 gpm (454 to 681 lpm)

Answer - D
Reference - FFS, p 553

39. What is an advantage of a fog-stream nozzle?
    A. Greater heat absorption per gallon discharged
    B. Lower operating pressure
    C. Less disruption of thermal layering
    D. Longer stream reach

Answer - A
Reference - FFS, p 569

40. Compared to fog nozzle streams, smooth-bore nozzle streams:
    A. Are more effective for hydraulic ventilation
    B. Absorb less heat
    C. Cause more disruption of thermal layering
    D. Have a lower discharge volume

Answer - B
Reference - FFS, p 569

Chapter 17

41. Prior to advancing a hoseline into a burning area, firefighters operating the hose should be _____ of the door.
    A. Kneeling or crouching directly in front
    B. Standing directly in front
    C. Lying flat in front
    D. Crouching or kneeling while positioned to the side.

Answer - D
Reference - FFS, p 562

42. The elements needed to produce quality firefighting mechanical foam include:
    A. Proportioner, CO_2, and educator
    B. Air, concentrate, educator, CO_2
    C. Aspiration, subsurface injection, and air
    D. Air, water, and concentrate

Answer - B
Reference - FFS, p 573

43. Application rate in relationship to a flammable liquids fire is:
    A. Ratio of foam to water to generate an effective foam blanket
    B. Ratio of air to water needed to extinguish a fire
    C. Amount of foam or foam solution needed to extinguish a fire
    D. Amount of water needed to extinguish a fire

Answer - C
Reference - FFS, p 576

44. To produce the proper rate of foam on flammable liquids, a(n) is necessary.
    A. Aspirating tip
    B. High-volume pump
    C. Proportioner
    D. Fog nozzle

Answer - C
Reference - FFS, p 576

45. An advantage of Class A foam is that it:
   A. Is designed to self-seal on a liquid surface
   B. Allows water to penetrate dense materials instead of running off the surface
   C. Can be used on both Class A and Class B fires, in varying proportions
   D. Is designed to resist hydrocarbons

Answer - B
Reference - FFS, p 573

Notes on Fire Attack and Foam

Foam
   1. Several types of fire
   2. Prevent ignition
   3. Neutralize hazardous materials
   4. Produced by mixing foam concentrate with water and air
   5. Limitations - Will evaporate while it is being put down if the fire is too hot. Applied at much shorter ranges than water

Class A foam
   1. Ordinary combustibles
   2. Increases effectiveness of water by reducing surface tension
   3. 0.1% to 1% concentration
   4. Wet foam penetrates well
   5. Stiff foam is more effective when applied for protecting buildings
   6. Typically use 0.3-0.5% foam to water proportion

Class B foam
   1. Separates fuel from fire
   2. Do not disturb foam blanket
   3. Apply to flammable liquid spills to prevent fire
   4. Concentration 3% or 6% solution
   5. Do not mix different types of foam
   6. Major categories - protein, fluoroprotein, aqueous film forming (AFFF), alcohol resistant
   7. Use class B form for aircraft (Special K)

Foam equipment
   1. Foam eductor draws foam concentration from a container into a moving stream of water
   2. Foam injector adds the foam concentrate to the water stream under pressure.
   3. Do not put the foam mixer at the end of the nozzle, put it farther back (50-100 ft) so that you can more easily move the nozzle. This will also help prevent inadvertent disconnection.
   4. Batch mixing - concentrate poured directly into a booster tank

5. Premixing - place foam into 2.5-gal extinguisher 90% filled with water, then pressurize with compressed air.

Foam application
1. Portable extinguishers, handlines, master stream devices, fixed systems (sprinklers, aircraft hangars)
2. Low, medium, and high expansion (argon is remarkably high expanding)
3. Sweep method (roll on) - used on flammable product on open ground
4. Bankshot - used at fir where there is an object that can be used to deflect the foam stream
5. Rain down method - especially HAZMAT situations
6. If the flow of foam is interrupted, the fire will destroy the foam that has been applied

Foam apparatus
Airports
1. Large vehicles that are designed to quickly apply large quantities of form to flammable liquid fires
2. Remote control monitors can be used to apply foam will vehicle is in motion.
3. Foam trailers can shoot foam hundreds of feet.

Chapter 18
Firefighter Survival – Not included

Chapter 19
Salvage and Overhaul

1. After being run at load, generator should be run at idle speed for at least _____ before shutting down.
   A. 15 seconds
   B. 30 seconds
   C. 1 minute
   D. 2 minutes

Answer - D
Reference - FFS, p 615

2. A fire cannot be considered fully extinguished until _____ is complete.
   A. Loss control
   B. Overhaul
   C. Secondary search
   D. Suppression operation

Answer – B
Reference - FFS, p 612

3. If individual sprinkler heads cannot be shut off, what should be done to stop the flow of water?
   A. Close the water service valve at the water meter
   B. Open the fire department connection outside
   C. Close the sprinkler control valve
   D. Open the system drain valve

Answer – C
Reference - FFS, p 618

4. Which of the following is a portable electrical power source?
   A. Generator
   B. Alternator
   C. Inverter
   D. Transformer

Answer – A
Reference - FFS, p 614

Salvage and Overhaul

5. How much does water weigh?
   A. 7.5 lb. per gallon (3.4 kg per liter)
   B. 8.3 lb. per gallon (3.8 kg per liter)
   C. 10.5 lb. per gallon (4.8 kg per liter)
   D. 12.2 lb. per gallon (5.5 kg per liter)

Answer - B
Reference - FFS, p 617

6. What is a common location for a post indicator valve?
   A. On an exterior wall
   B. Next to the water meter
   C. On the main system riser
   D. In a utility or mechanical room

Answer - A
Reference - FFS, p 619

7. It is permissible to remove SCBA during salvage operations after:
   A. The atmosphere has been tested and found safe
   B. The area is clear of smoke
   C. All remaining fire has been extinguished
   D. The fire is extinguished

Answer – A
Reference - FFS, p 618

8. Which statement about the use of inverters is correct?
   A. Inverters must be used in a well-ventilated area.
   B. Inverters must be used in tandem with a generator.
   C. Inverters can be carried to areas that are inaccessible to vehicles.
   D. Power output is limited.

Answer – D
Reference - FFS, p 614

Chapter 19

9. Where do salvage operations usually begin?
   A. On the floor below the fire floor
   B. In high-value areas
   C. In the least damaged area
   D. As close to the seat of the fire as possible

Answer – D
Reference - FFS, p

10. Which of the following is the best option for extinguishing hot spots during overhaul?
    A. 2.5-gallon water or Class A fire extinguisher
    B. Medium-diameter hose line
    C. Booster line
    D. Small-diameter hose line

Answer – D
Reference - FFS, p 635

11. Operating a PIV handle is similar to operating a:
    A. Nozzle bale
    B. Pump panel pull-valve
    C. Hydrant wrench
    D. Ball valve

Answer – C
Reference - FFS, p 620

12. Which hazard is of particular concern during salvage?
    A. Unnecessary water damage
    B. Fire in void spaces
    C. Structural collapse
    D. Rekindle

Answer – C
Reference - FFS, p 617

Salvage and Overhaul

13. What is a common salvage operation?
    A. Utility control
    B. Covering ventilation openings
    C. Pulling ceilings
    D. Determining the cause and origin of the fire

Answer – A
Reference - FFS, p 617

14. A long section of protective material used to protect flooring or carpet is a:
    A. Floor roll
    B. Salvage mat
    C. Carpet cover
    D. Floor runner

Answer – D
Reference - FFS, p 631

15. What should be done when a small tear is found in a salvage cover?
    A. Return the cover to the manufacturer for repair
    B. Repair the tear with a vulcanizing-type patch
    C. Remove the cover from service
    D. Apply duct tape over the tear

Answer – D
Reference - FFS, p 628

16. How is a sprinkler wedge used to stop flow from an activated sprinkler?
    A. Insert the wedge into the orifice and drive it into place with a striking tool
    B. Tap a wedge into place between the orifice and the deflector
    C. Tap two wedges into place above and below the deflector
    D. Push two wedges together from opposite sides between the orifice and the deflector

Answer – D
Reference - FFS, p 618

Chapter 19

17. Which item is commonly used to improvise a water chute?
    A. Hard suction hose
    B. Water vacuum
    C. Attic ladder
    D. Salvage cover

Answer – D
Reference - FFS, p 623

18. What is the most reliable method for determining whether there is hidden fire?
    A. Direct inspection
    B. Thermal imaging
    C. Odor/sight of smoke
    D. Atmospheric modeling

Answer – A
Reference - FFS, p 635

19. Which hazard is of particular concern when running an electrical generator in an enclosed space?
    A. Hearing protection
    B. Grounding
    C. Ventilation
    D. Heat from the exhaust system

Answer – C
Reference - FFS, p 614

20. What is the term for operations undertaken to limit or reduce property loss?
    A. Salvage
    B. Overhaul
    C. Recovery
    D. Loss control

Answer – A
Reference - FFS, p 612

Salvage and Overhaul

21. When should a sprinkler system be shut down?
    A. Prior to beginning salvage operations
    B. When overhaul is complete
    C. When the IC declares the fire to be under control
    D. Upon connection to the FDC

Answer – C
Reference - FFS, p 618

22. Which walls are usually opened first during overhaul?
    A. The most heavily damaged walls
    B. The least damaged walls
    C. Walls with chases
    D. Partition walls

Answer – A
Reference - FFS, p 637

23. What is a limitation of backpack water vacuums?
    A. Lift is limited to approximately three feet
    B. They cannot be worn with SCBA
    C. They must be used in a well-ventilated area
    D. They cannot be used with dirty water

Answer – B
Reference - FFS, p 624

24. Which items are best overhauled outside the structure?
    A. Appliances
    B. Books/documents
    C. Furniture
    D. Clothing wardrobe

Answer – C
Reference - FFS, p 635

Chapter 19

25. Which statement about the use of a thermal imager during overhaul operations is correct?
    A. A thermal imager is particularly useful for scanning through heavy insulating materials.
    B. Some ambient light is required for the unit to produce a useful image.
    C. Imagers used for search and rescue should not be used for overhaul.
    D. The imager depicts the temperature differential between an object and its surroundings.

Answer - D
Reference - FFS, p 635

26. A threaded stem indicates the valve position on which sprinkler control valve?
    A. Outside stem and yoke
    B. Post indicator
    C. Gate
    D. Butterfly

Answer – A
Reference - FFS, p 619

27. During salvage, what is the best way to suddenly stop the flow from a single sprinkler head?
    A. Close the branch line valve
    B. Replace the bulb or link
    C. Insert a sprinkler wedge
    D. Install a replacement head

Answer – C
Reference - FFS, p 618

28. Which tool will be needed to shut off a main sprinkler control valve without the necessary key?
    A. Vise-grips
    B. A pipe wrench
    C. A pry bar
    D. Bolt cutters

Answer – D
Reference - FFS, p 619

Salvage and Overhaul

29. Ideally, when should overhaul operations begin?
   A. As soon as resources are available
   B. After fire investigators have examined the scene
   C. Any time after extinguishment
   D. Concurrently with salvage

Answer – D
Reference - FFS, p 612

30. If overhaul operations may disturb possible evidence, what should fire fighters do before continuing with their work?
   A. Have a law enforcement officer evaluate the situation
   B. Take photos or make sketches of the evidence in an undisturbed state
   C. Tag and bag the evidence
   D. Wait for investigators to examine it

Answer – B
Reference - FFS, p 633

31. A gasoline-powered generator should be test-run for ___ minutes.
   A. 5 to 10
   B. 5 to 15
   C. 10 to 15
   D. 15 to 30

Answer – D
Reference - FFS, p 615

32. Which type of light projects a diffuse light over a wide area?
   A. Flood
   B. Spot
   C. Halogen
   D. LED

Answer – A
Reference - FFS, p 612

33. During salvage, what should be done with any pictures on the walls?
   A. They should be left in place and covered with plastic sheeting
   B. They should be left in place and turned toward the wall
   C. They should be removed and placed with the furniture
   D. They should be placed face-down under a bed

Answer - C
Reference - FFS, p 626

34. Which device interrupts the current when there is a problem with an electrical ground?
   A. ECB
   B. EGR
   C. GCI
   D. GFI

Answer - D
Reference - FFS, p 612

35. The output range for portable lights is generally ____ watts:
   A. 250 to 500
   B. 500 to 750
   C. 500 to 1000
   D. 300 to 1500

Answer - D
Reference - FFS, p 613

Chapter 20
Firefighter Rehabilitation

1. The USFA recommends establishing a rehabilitation operation when the heat stress index reaches:
   A. 80°F (27°C)
   B. 85°F (29°C)
   C. 90°F (32°C)
   D. 95°F (35°C)

Answer - C
Reference - FFS, p 651

2. Drinks that contain _____ should be avoided for fluid replacement.
   A. electrolytes
   B. sugar
   C. caffeine
   D. Salt

Answer - C
Reference - FFS, p 653

3. In which type of incident is the rehab center located farthest from the operational area?
   A. High-rise
   B. Wildland
   C. Confined space
   D. Hazardous materials

Answer - B
Reference - FFS, p

4. At which types of incidents is rehabilitation a concern?
   A. High-intensity/long-duration incidents
   B. Incidents requiring the use of full PPE
   C. All fire incidents
   D. All incidents

Answer - D
Reference - FFS, p 648

Chapter 20

5. During short-duration incidents, which type of nourishment is ideal for fire fighters to sustain peak performance levels?
   A. Low-sugar, high-protein sports bars
   B. Equal portions of protein, carbohydrate, and fat
   C. Caffeinated soda
   D. Plain water only

Answer - A
Reference - FFS, p 655

6. How does PPE prevent evaporative cooling?
   A. The liner reflects evaporative heat
   B. Perspiration is absorbed in the layers
   C. The thermal barrier prevents heat transfer
   D. The vapor barrier prevents evaporation of sweat.

Answer - D
Reference - FFS, p 645

7. What is the most common source of saturated fats?
   A. Animal products
   B. Dark-leaf vegetables
   C. Cereal grains
   D. Fish

Answer - A
Reference - FFS, p 655

8. In the time it takes to consume two SCBA air cylinders, enough body fluid can be lost to result in:
   A. Impaired temperature regulation
   B. Heat exhaustion
   C. Heat stroke
   D. Syncope

Answer - A
Reference - FFS, p 653

9. A PPE ensemble weighs at least _____.
   A. 25 lb. (11kg)
   B. 40 lb. (18 kg)
   C. 60 lb. (27 kg)
   D. 75 lb. (34 kg)

Answer - B
Reference - FFS, p 645

10. Fats should account for approximately what percent of calories in a balanced diet:
    A. 10 to 15 percent
    B. 25 to 30 percent
    C. 40 to 50 percent
    D. 55 to 65 percent

Answer - B
Reference - FFS, p 655

11. What is a common sign or symptom of high blood glucose?
    A. Syncope
    B. Profuse sweating
    C. Sluggish feeling
    D. Nausea/vomiting

Answer – C
Reference - FFS, p 654

12. Which of the following is a form of passive cooling?
    A. Rest in an air-conditioned environment
    B. Use of misting fans
    C. Immersion in cool water
    D. Application of wet towels

Answer – A
Reference - FFS, p 652

Chapter 20

13. At five percent dehydration, work capacity can be decreased by as much as:
    A. 5 percent
    B. 10 percent
    C. 20 percent
    D. 30 percent

Answer - D
Reference - FFS, p 647

14. What is an ideal location for the rehabilitation center at a high-rise fire?
    A. In a safe location on the fire floor
    B. Two or three floors below the fire
    C. In the lobby of the fire building
    D. Outside but nearby the fire building

Answer – B
Reference - FFS, p 650

15. What is the body's primary source of energy?
    A. Glucose
    B. Insulin
    C. Electrolytes
    D. Protein

Answer - A
Reference - FFS, p 654

16. Carbohydrates should account for approximately _____ of calories in a balanced diet.
    A. 30 percent
    B. 45 percent
    C. 60 percent
    D. 75 percent

Answer - C
Reference - FFS, p 654

17. How are rehabilitation concerns affected by cold weather?
    A. Rehab should include access to dry clothing
    B. PPE reduces the likelihood of hypothermia
    C. Drinking hot liquids should be prohibited
    D. Recommended fluid intake is reduced

Answer - A
Reference - FFS, p 652

18. Which condition is defined as an internal body temperature less than 95°F (35°C)?
    A. Chilblains
    B. Hypothermia
    C. Frost bite
    D. Exposure

Answer - B
Reference - FFS, p 651

19. What is the best source of complex carbohydrates?
    A. Whole-grain bread
    B. Fish
    C. Red meat
    D. Vegetables

Answer - A
Reference - FFS, p 655

20. How are rehabilitation concerns affected by high humidity?
    A. Time spent is rehab can be reduced
    B. Rehab time must be doubled
    C. The likelihood of hypothermia increases with humidity
    D. Regulation of body temperature is more difficult

Answer - D
Reference - FFS, p

Chapter 20

21. Safety begins with _____.
    A. Realistic training
    B. Developing good habits
    C. Taking personal responsibility
    D. Leadership by example

Answer - C
Reference - FFS, p 656

22. Personal protective equipment has the greatest effect on which body function?
    A. Perfusion
    B. Respiration
    C. Temperature regulation
    D. Cellular metabolism

Answer - C
Reference - FFS, p 645

23. The amount of rest needed to recover from physical exertion is related to the intensity of the work performed.
    A. Somewhat
    B. Directly
    C. Inversely
    D. Not

Answer - B
Reference - FFS, p

24. Hypothermia is defined as a body temperature less than:
    A. 89 F (32 C)
    B. 91 F (33 C)
    C. 93 F (34 C)
    D. 95 F (35 C)

Answer - D
Reference - FFS, p 651

25. What is the most reliable way to stay well hydrated?
    A. Use urine color as an indicator of hydration
    B. Drink as much as you can during work periods
    C. Drink early and often
    D. Drink when you are thirsty

Answer - C
Reference - FFS, p 653

26. Which of the following is a form of active cooling?
    A. Rest in an air-conditioned environment
    B. Removal of PPE
    C. Rest in a shady area
    D. Application of wet, cool towels

Answer - D
Reference - FFS, p 652

27. What does the SAID (specific adaptation to imposed demands) principle apply to?
    A. Training methods
    B. Critical incident stress
    C. Rehabilitation
    D. Tactics and strategy

Answer - A
Reference - FFS, p 645

28. According to the NFPA, rehab should be required after a fire fighter has consumed _____ 30-minute SCBA bottles(s).

    A. 1
    B. 2
    C. 3
    D. 4

Answer - B
Reference - FFS, p 656

Chapter 20

29. Which statement about rehabilitation is correct?
    A. Rehab should be limited to high-intensity or long-duration incidents.
    B. The need for rehab should be determined by line personnel.
    C. A rehab center should be established at every incident.
    D. Rehab should be a consideration on every incident.

Answer - D
Reference - FFS, p 648

30. How should fire fighters be released from rehabilitation?
    A. Individuals should be released as they complete the rehab process
    B. Personnel should be released on an as-needed basis
    C. Personnel should check out in the same order that they checked in
    D. All members of a crew should be released together

Answer - D
Reference - FFS, p 656

31. The most serious consequences of untreated dehydration is:
    A. Heat exhaustion
    B. Heat stroke
    C. Death
    D. Syncope

Answer - C
Reference - FFS, p 646

32. The danger category of the heat stress index is determined by the:
    A. Apparent temperature
    B. Relative humidity
    C. Air temperature
    D. Duration of exposure

Answer - A
Reference - FFS, p 647

Firefightter Rehabilitation

33. Which of the following activities produces the highest level of physiological stress?
    A. Working in a fully encapsulated suit
    B. A medical emergency where the victim is choking
    C. Vehicle accident requiring extrication
    D. Back-to-back incidents

Answer – A
Reference - FFS, p

34. What is a common sign or symptom of low blood sugar?
    A. Excessive thirst
    B. Feeling weak and shaky
    C. Muscle cramps
    D. Nausea and vomiting

Answer - B
Reference - FFS, p 654

35. What is the main component in tissue growth and repair?
    A. Carbohydrates
    B. Lipids
    C. Unsaturated fats
    D. Protein

Answer - D
Reference - FFS, p 655

36. When does the rest phase begin during the rehabilitation process?
    A. After rehydration and calorie replacement
    B. After the initial medical evaluation
    C. Upon arrival at the rehabilitation center
    D. After body temperature has been restored.

Answer - C
Reference - FFS, p 652

37. At which types of incidents should a rehabilitation center be established?
    A. High-intensity/long-duration incidents
    B. Incidents requiring the use of full PPE
    C. All fire incidents
    D. All incidents

Answer - D
Reference - FFS, p 648, 651

38. Protein should account for approximately _____ of calories in a balanced diet.
    A. 10 percent
    B. 25 percent
    C. 40 percent
    D. 55 percent

Answer - A
Reference - FFS, p 655

39. Who plans ahead to make sure there is a fresh or rested crew ready to rotate with a crew that needs rehabilitation?
    A. The staging officer
    B. The company officer
    C. The incident commander
    D. The logistics section chief

Answer - C
Reference - FFS, p 650

40. How should crew members check into the rehab center?
    A. Individually
    B. All members together
    C. In assigned pairs
    D. On an as-needed basis

Answer - B
Reference - FFS, p 656

Chapter 21
Wildland and Ground Fires

1. Subsurface fuels are challenging to deal with because they are:
    A. Highly susceptible to changes in weather
    B. Continuous
    C. Readily ignitable
    D. Hard to locate

Answer - D
Reference - FFS, p 663

2. What is the last resort for a fire fighter in danger of being overrun by a wildland fire?
    A. Flee to the safety zone
    B. Take shelter in a house
    C. Deploy a fire shelter
    D. Take shelter in a vehicle cab

Answer - C
Reference - FFS, p 672

3. What is another term for aerial fuels?
    A. Raised
    B. Ladder
    C. Canopy
    D. Elevated

Answer - C
Reference - FFS, p 663

4. If a wildland or ground cover fire is too dangerous for a direct attack, which type of fire attack should be used?
    A. Head
    B. Pincer
    C. Indirect
    D. Ranking

Answer - C
Reference - FFS, p 669

5. Which factor has the greatest effect on the moisture content of fuels?
   A. Continuity
   B. Wind
   C. Temperature
   D. Relative humidity

Answer - D
Reference - FFS, p 665

6. Which of the following is an example of a fine fuel?
   A. Root
   B. Stick
   C. Branch
   D. Grass

Answer - D
Reference - FFS, p 663

7. What is the term for the partly decomposed organic material on a forest floor?
   A. Understory
   B. Litter
   C. Surface compost
   D. Ground duff

Answer - D
Reference - FFS, p 663

8. Ground cover is an example of a(n) _____ fuel.
   A. Surface
   B. Understory
   C. Compact
   D. Live

Answer - A
Reference - FFS, p 663

9. The unburned part of a wildland fire area is the:
    A. Island
    B. Clear
    C. Perimeter
    D. Green

Answer - A
Reference - FFS, p 666

10. In which type of fuel will a fire spread the most rapidly?
    A. Compacted
    B. Brush
    C. Slash
    D. Fine

Answer - D
Reference - FFS, p 663

11. What is one of the three categories of wildland fire causes?
    A. Proximal
    B. Mechanical
    C. Natural
    D. Electrical

Answer - C
Reference - FFS, p 664

12. What is the area between the fingers of a wildland fire?
    A. Peninsula
    B. Pocket
    C. Island
    D. Joint

Answer - B
Reference - FFS, p 666

13. Wildland fuels that lie under the surface of the ground are _____ fuels.
    A. Subsurface
    B. Understory
    C. Duff
    D. Substory

Answer - A
Reference - FFS, p 663

14. What is the term for a long, narrow extension of fire projecting out from the main body of a wildland fire?
    A. Island
    B. spot
    C. Run
    D. Finger

Answer - D
Reference - FFS, p 666

15. What is another term for surface fuels?
    A. Litter
    B. Duff
    C. Ground
    D. Understory

Answer - C
Reference - FFS, p 663

16. Which NFPA standard covers wildland fire fighter professional qualifications?
    A. 1051
    B. 1041
    C. 1031
    D. 1021

Answer - A
Reference - FFS, p 674

17. Which federal government agency manages wildland incidents occurring on federal lands?
    A. Occupational Health and Safety Administration
    B. Federal Emergency Management Agency
    C. U.S. Forest Service
    D. U.S. Fire Administration

Answer - C
Reference - FFS, p 662

18. The smothering method of extinguishment is most frequently used in which wildland operation?
    A. Direct attack
    B. Cold trailing
    C. Indirect attack
    D. Overhaul

Answer - D
Reference - FFS, p 667

19. Which condition will generally result in lower relative humidity?
    A. Higher fuel moisture
    B. Precipitation
    C. Nighttime
    D. Increasing temperature

Answer - D
Reference - FFS, p 665

20. What is slash?
    A. Partially decomposed organic matter
    B. Debris from logging or clearing operations
    C. Seasonal ground cover
    D. Partially burned fuel

Answer - B
Reference - FFS, p 663

Chapter 21

21. What is one of the ten standard wildland firefighting orders?
    A. Base all actions on current and expected fire behavior
    B. Do not attempt to outrun a fire uphill
    C. Focus on what is not burning, rather than what is burning
    D. Attack the flanks of the fire, not the head

Answer - A
Reference - FFS, p 674

22. What is the term for the natural and human-made features of land?
    A. Cartography
    B. Geography
    C. Topography
    D. Geology

Answer - C
Reference - FFS, p 665

23. Fuels that are in contact with each other are described as:
    A. Uninterrupted
    B. Continuous
    C. Compact
    D. Unbroken

Answer - B
Reference - FFS, p 664

24. The most rapidly moving part of a wildland fire is the:
    A. Foot
    B. Apex
    C. Head
    D. Point

Answer - C
Reference - FFS, p 666

25. Which extinguishing agent is best suited for use in wildland fire operations?
    A. Compressed-air foam
    B. AFFF
    C. Dry chemical
    D. Carbon dioxide

Answer - A
Reference - FFS, p 667

26. What is one of the two primary methods of direct attack on a wildland fire?
    A. Pincer
    B. Frontal
    C. Backfire
    D. Aerial

Answer - A
Reference - FFS, p 668

27. What is the ratio of water in air compared to the maximum amount of water vapor the air can hold at a given temperature?
    A. Saturation index
    B. Relative humidity
    C. Barometric pressure
    D. Moisture ratio

Answer - B
Reference - FFS, p 665

28. Which NFPA standard covers protective clothing and equipment for wildland firefighting?
    A. 1977
    B. 1978
    C. 1979
    D. 1980

Answer - A
Reference - FFS, p 672

Chapter 21

29. Which type of wildland fire attack is made on the fire's burning edge?
    A. Direct
    B. Offensive
    C. Frontal
    D. Indirect

Answer - A
Reference - FFS, p 667

30. What is a characteristic of fine fuels?
    A. Large surface area relative to volume
    B. Resistance to rapid changes in fuel moisture
    C. Long burn duration
    D. Difficulty in extinguishing them

Answer - A
Reference - FFS, p 663

31. Why do compact fuels burn slowly?
    A. They have less surface area
    B. Air cannot circulate as freely
    C. They retain moisture
    D. They are less continuous

Answer - B
Reference - FFS, p 663

32. What is dry lightning?
    A. A lightning strike that does not cause fire
    B. Lightning without rain
    C. Lightning occurring in otherwise fair weather
    D. Lightning that does not contact the ground

Answer - B
Reference - FFS, p 664

33. Which type of respiratory protection is normally used in wildland firefighting?
    A. SCBA
    B. Filter mask
    C. APR
    D. PAPR

Answer - B
Reference - FFS, p 672

34. Which tool combines an axe with an adze?
    A. Brush hook
    B. Pulaski
    C. McLeod
    D. Council rake

Answer - B
Reference - FFS, p 666

35. On which basis are wildland fuels classified?
    A. Weight
    B. Diameter
    C. Moisture content
    D. Composition

Answer - B
Reference - FFS, p 663

36. The quantity of wildland fuel available in a specific area is fuel _____.
    A. Loading
    B. Volume
    C. Continuity
    D. Density

Answer - B
Reference - FFS, p 664

37. The NFPA defines wildland fires as unplanned and uncontrolled fires burning in _____ fuel.
    A. Organic
    B. Vegetative
    C. Living
    D. Natural

Answer - B
Reference - FFS, p 662

38. The majority of ground cover fires are extinguished with which item?
    A. CAFS
    B. Aircraft
    C. Backpack pump
    D. Backfire

Answer - C
Reference - FFS, p 666

39. Which of the following is a component of the wildland fire triangle?
    A. Heat
    B. Humidity
    C. Fuel moisture
    D. Wind

Answer - A
Reference - FFS, p 662

40. The maximum diameter of a 1-hour fuel is _____.
    A. 1/4" (6 mm)
    B. 1/2" (13 mm)
    C. 3/4" (19 mm)
    D. 1" (25 mm)

Answer - A
Reference - FFS, p 663

Wildland and Ground Fires

41. What is one of the ten standard wildland firefighting orders?
    A. Avoid downhill fire line construction
    B. Establish and maintain chain of command and span of control
    C. Keep informed on weather conditions and forecasts
    D. Beware of unburned fuel between you and the fire

Answer - C
Reference - FFS, p 674

42. Which term means areas where undeveloped land with vegetative fuels is mixed with human-made structures?
    A. Rural—urban intermix
    B. Rural development zone
    C. Greenbelt
    D. Wildland—urban interface

Answer - D
Reference - FFS, p 674

43. The distance between fire fighters in a safety zone and the flames should be a minimum of _____ times the flame height.
    A. 2
    B. 3
    C. 4
    D. 5

Answer - C
Reference - FFS, p 672

44. What does the "E" in LCES stand for?
    A. Establish lookouts
    B. Expect surprises
    C. Establish accountability
    D. Escape routes

Answer - D
Reference - FFS, p 665

Chapter 21

45. Which tool is a combination of hoe and rake?
   A. Pulaski
   B. Forestry hoe
   C. Combination

Answer - D
Reference - FFS, p 666

Notes on Wildland and Ground Fires

Fuel types
   1. Fine - one-hour fuels, less than ¼ inch diameter, grass, leaves, tree moss, and loose surface litter.
   2. Light - ten-hour fuels, ¼ inch to one-inch diameter, small twigs, and stems
   3. Medium - hundred-hour fuels, one inch to three inches
   4. Coarse and heavily compacted fuels - 1000-hour fuels, three-inch diameter or greater, logs
   5. Locations - Subsurface, surface, and aerial fuels

Types of attack
   1. Direct - two crews mount a two-pronged attack to pinch the fire out at its shoulders, extinguishing the fire at its burning edge
   2. Indirect - one crew attacks one side of the fire

Chapter 22
Fire Suppression

1. What is the target of the hose stream in an indirect attack?
    A. The base of the fire
    B. The ceiling of the fire room
    C. As close to the fire as possible
    D. The most threatened exposure

Answer - B
Reference - FFS, p 685

2. Which of the following is an example of a two-dimensional fire?
    A. Ground cover fire
    B. Flammable liquid spill on open ground
    C. Roof fire
    D. Fire contained within a void space

Answer - B
Reference - FFS, p 699

3. What is an advantage of a straight stream over a fog stream?
    A. Greater heat absorption
    B. Longer reach
    C. Increased surface area of the stream
    D. Less nozzle reaction

Answer - B
Reference - FFS, p 684

4. What is the correct method to stop the flow of gas delivered via utility pipeline into a structure?
    A. Delegate the task to the utility company
    B. Close the valve on the cylinder
    C. Pinch the pipe closed using grounded pipe clamps
    D. Turn off the valve at the meter

Answer - B
Reference - FFS, p 701

5. What happens during a blitz attack?
   A. A master stream is used for an offensive operation
   B. Opposing hose lines are used in a coordinated attack
   C. Fire attack is made regardless of ventilation status
   D. The building of origin is considered unsavable

Answer - A
Reference - FFS, p 682

6. What is the correct method to stop the flow of gas into a structure supplied by an outside storage cylinder?
   A. Rotate the quarter-turn valve at the meter
   B. Close the valve on the cylinder
   C. Disconnect the cylinder
   D. Delegate the task to the gas service company

Answer - B
Reference - FFS, p 700

7. If there is no life-safety hazard, which type of fire attack should be used in a building under construction?
   A. Blitz
   B. Indirect
   C. Offensive
   D. Defensive

Answer - D
Reference - FFS, p 694

8. Defensive firefighting operations are conducted from which location?
   A. Interior
   B. Roof
   C. Exterior
   D. Exposure

Answer - C
Reference - FFS, p 680

9. What it the maximum diameter of a small handline?
   A. 1 ½" (38mm)
   B. 1 ¾" (45 mm)
   C. 2" (50 mm)
   D. 2 1/2" (65 mm)

Answer - C
Reference - FFS, p 683

10. How should fire fighters approach a vehicle fire?
    A. 90° angle from the side
    B. 45° angle from the side
    C. Directly from the front
    D. Directly from the rear

Answer - B
Reference - FFS, p 697

11. If it is necessary to approach a horizontal flammable-gas cylinder, you should approach _____.
    A. From a 45° angle to the side
    B. From either end
    C. Perpendicular (90° angle) to the side
    D. Via the shortest, most direct route

Answer - C
Reference - FFS, p 701

12. Which term refers to two crews operating hose lines against each other?
    A. Opposing hose lines
    B. Combination attack
    C. Freelancing
    D. Uncoordinated attack

Answer - A
Reference - FFS, p 683

Chapter 22

13. In which type of operation are large handlines and master streams more often used?
    A. Defensive
    B. Offensive
    C. Indirect
    D. Tactical

Answer - A
Reference - FFS, p 681

14. Which hazardous material is commonly found in vehicle batteries?
    A. Hydrochloric acid
    B. Hydrofluoric acid
    C. Sulfuric acid
    D. Pentaic acid

Answer – C
Reference - FFS, p 698

15. For which type of operations are master stream devices most commonly used?
    A. Offensive
    B. Defensive
    C. Combination
    D. Blitz

Answer – B
Reference - FFS, p 681

16. What is a potential problem associated with an indirect fire attack?
    A. Pushing the fire into uninvolved areas
    B. Unnecessary water damage
    C. Increased likelihood of opposing hose streams
    D. Displacement of hot fire gases toward the floor

Answer – D
Reference - FFS, p

Fire Suppression

17. When water is convened to steam, it expands to _____ times the volume of an equivalent amount of liquid water.
    A. 1600
    B. 1700
    C. 1800
    D. 1900

Answer – B
Reference - FFS, p

18. Master streams are most commonly used for _____ attack.
    A. Defensive
    B. Offensive
    C. Direct
    D. Indirect

Answer – A
Reference - FFS, p 681

19. Which type of attack is used when the main objective is to protect exposures?
    A. Indirect
    B. Offensive
    C. Defensive
    D. Tactical

Answer – C
Reference - FFS, p 681

20. A combination fire attack begins with _____.
    A. An exterior attack
    B. An indirect attack
    C. Exposure protection
    D. Ventilation

Answer – B
Reference - FFS, p 686

Chapter 22

21. Which hazard is of particular concern with fires involving stacked or piled material?
    A. Collapse
    B. Rekindle
    C. Interference with sprinkler systems
    D. Toxic exposure

Answer – A
Reference - FFS, p 695

22. When directing the flow of water from the nozzle during a combination attack, where should the flow of water first be directed?
    A. Lower-left corner of the fire
    B. Lower-right corner of the fire
    C. Upper-left corner of the fire
    D. Upper-right corner of the fire

Answer – C
Reference - FFS, p 686

23. Which fire-extinguishing agent would be the best choice for use on delicate electronic equipment?
    A. Ordinary dry chemical
    B. Multipurpose dry chemical
    C. Aqueous film-forming foam (AFFF)
    D. Carbon dioxide

Answer – D
Reference - FFS, p 702

24. Which hazard presents the greatest risk for a fire in a modern vehicle?
    A. Bursting tires
    B. Exploding fuel tanks
    C. Components containing pressurized gas
    D. Laminated glass

Answer – C
Reference - FFS, p 696

Fire Suppression

25. Which item is installed on propane cylinders to allow excess pressure to escape?
    A. Frangible plug
    B. Blowout disk
    C. Purge valve
    D. Relief valve

Answer – D
Reference - FFS, p 700

26. Which cancer-causing material do transformers contain?
    A. Polyphenyl chlorinates
    B. Biphenyl chlorinates
    C. Polychlorinated vinyls
    D. Polychlorinated biphenyls

Answer – D
Reference - FFS, p 702

27. What is the objective of an indirect fire attack?
    A. Exposure protection
    B. Rapid cooling of the atmosphere
    C. Containment of the fire to the building of origin
    D. Occupant protection

Answer – B
Reference - FFS, p 685

28. Operations are conducted from outside of the fire building in which operational mode?
    A. Rescue
    B. Offensive
    C. Defensive
    D. Tactical

Answer – C
Reference - FFS, p 680

Chapter 22

29. When is an indirect attack indicated?
    A. When the structure is badly weakened
    B. When exposures are immediately threatened
    C. With an incipient fire
    D. When flashover is likely

Answer – D
Reference - FFS, p 685

30. What is the most severe hazard associated with propane products?
    A. Asphyxiation
    B. BLEVE
    C. Cryogenic injury
    D. Fuel leak

Answer – B
Reference - FFS, p 700

31. Portable monitors, deck guns, and ladder pipes are examples of _____.
    A. Handlines
    B. Aerial streams
    C. Deluge sets
    D. Master stream devices

Answer – D
Reference - FFS, p 687

32. What is the minimum number of fire fighters needed to advance and maneuver a 2 ½" (65-mm) handline inside a building?
    A. 1
    B. 2
    C. 3
    D. 4

Answer – C
Reference - FFS, p 686

Fire Suppression

33. What is the best item to aid extinguishment of smoldering fires in tightly packed combustible materials?
    A. Class A foam
    B. Piercing nozzle
    C. Water fog
    D. Dry chemical

Answer – A
Reference - FFS, p 695

34. How much risk to fire fighters' lives is acceptable in attempting to minimize damage to property that is already severely damaged?
    A. None
    B. A little
    C. A moderate amount
    D. A lot

Answer – A
Reference - FFS, p

35. What is the target of the hose stream in a direct attack?
    A. The base of the fire
    B. Hot overhead gases
    C. Exposure surfaces
    D. The most threatened exposure

Answer – A
Reference - FFS, p 685

36. What is added to propane to give it a distinct odor?
    A. Mercaptan
    B. Triptan
    C. Sulfur
    D. Methane

Answer – A
Reference - FFS, p 700

37. What is the minimum flow from a master stream device?
   A. 350 gpm (1325 lpm)
   B. 450 gpm (1700 lpm)
   C. 500 gpm (1900 lpm)
   D. 750 gpm (2800 lpm)

Answer – A
Reference - FFS, p 683

38. What is the minimum size hose line for a vehicle fire?
   A. 1" (25 mm)
   B. 1 ½" (38 mm)
   C. 1 ¾" (45 mm)
   D. 2 ½" (65 mm)

Answer – B
Reference - FFS, p 696

39. Which type of fire attack has as its objective preventing the spread of fire?
   A. Defensive
   B. Offensive
   C. Direct
   D. Indirect

Answer – A
Reference - FFS, p 680

40. Large handlines flow approximately _____?
   A. 150 gpm (570 lpm)
   B. 200 gpm (760 lpm)
   C. 250 gpm (950 lpm)
   D. 350 gpm (1325 lpm)

Answer – C
Reference - FFS, p 683

Fire Suppression

41. What is a characteristic of a fog stream?
    A. It is ideal for reaching distant targets
    B. It produces minimal air turbulence
    C. It creates water droplets with a large surface area
    D. It produces less runoff than a solid stream

Answer – C
Reference - FFS, p 683

42. The use of master streams on a building should be prohibited if:
    A. A blitz attack is under way
    B. The primary search has not been completed
    C. Crews are working inside the building
    D. There is no threat to exposures

Answer C
Reference - FFS, p 687

43. A burning liquid that is pouring over the edge of a container is known as a _____ fire.
    A. Flowing
    B. Continuous
    C. Three-dimensional
    D. Cascading

Answer – C
Reference - FFS, p 699

44. Where should additional equipment be staged on a high-rise fire?
    A. On the floor above the fire floor
    B. On the ground floor
    C. One or two floors below the fire
    D. On the fire floor

Answer – C
Reference - FFS, p

Chapter 22

45. A master stream device that is permanently mounted on an engine and plumbed directly into the pump is a:
    A. Monitor
    B. Deck gun
    C. Playpipe
    D. deluge set

Answer – B
Reference - FFS, p 687

46. Why is it necessary to limit the lowest stream angle of a portable monitor?
    A. To ensure the safety of crews and equipment operating nearby
    B. To minimize flooding around the monitor
    C. To reduce stress on the supply lines
    D. To prevent instability of the monitor

Answer – A
Reference - FFS, p 690

47. Which statement about using hose streams on an elevated transformer fire is correct?
    A. You should use just enough water to cool, but not extinguish, the fire.
    B. Water should be applied in short bursts.
    C. This technique may cause splashing and spread of toxic liquids.
    D. Class B foam is the ideal extinguishing agent.

Answer – C
Reference - FFS, p 702

48. When approaching a burning flammable liquid vessel to operate the valve, which combination of hose streams should be used?
    A. One 1 ¾" (38 mm)
    B. Two 1 ¾" (38 mm)
    C. One 2 ½" (65 mm)
    D. Two 2 ½" (65 mm)

Answer – B
Reference - FFS, p 701

Fire Suppression

49. Close-range application of water to the fire is the objective of which type of operation?
   A. Combination
   B. Defensive
   C. Offensive
   D. Transitional

Answer – C
Reference - FFS, p 680

50. What is the most common hazard associated with confined spaces?
   A. Carcinogenic materials
   B. Atmospheric conditions
   C. Explosion
   D. Electrical shock

Answer – B
Reference - FFS, p 696

51. Where should streams be directed to prevent a BLEVE?
   A. On the relief valve
   B. At the tank ends
   C. At the area where the tank is being heated
   D. On the protective dome

Answer – C
Reference - FFS, p 700

52. Which statement about ventilating a basement fire is correct?
   A. Vertical ventilation is the preferred method.
   B. Ventilation must be accomplished as soon as possible.
   C. Ventilation is generally ineffective in basement fires.
   D. Fire attack should not be delayed while awaiting ventilation.

Answer – D
Reference - FFS, p 602

Chapter 22

53. When shutting down electrical service to a structure, you should:
   A. Apply a lockout device
   B. Remove the breakers
   C. Notify the utility company
   D. Test an outlet

Answer – A
Reference - FFS, p 701

54. A vehicle fueled by CNG or LPG is fully involved in fire. Which of the following should be used to fight the fire?
   A. Carbon dioxide
   B. 1 ¾" (45-mm) hose stream
   C. 2 ½" (65-mm) hose stream
   D. Unmanned master stream

Answer – D
Reference - FFS, p 697

55. An elevated master stream device mounted at the tip of an aerial ladder is a _____.
   A. Ladder pipe
   B. Turret
   C. Snorkel
   D. Rung gun

Answer – A
Reference - FFS, p 690

56. What is an indication that a hose stream has cooled ceiling-level gases?
   A. The atmosphere in the room clears
   B. The ceiling becomes plainly visible
   C. The smoke level drops to the floor
   D. Water droplets rain down

Answer – D
Reference - FFS, p 685

Fire Suppression

57. When can one fire fighter safely handle a large handline?
    A. When using a 50 psi (350 kPa) nozzle
    B. When using the handline for exposure protection
    C. Under no circumstances
    D. When the handline is stationary and well anchored

Answer – D
Reference - FFS, p 683

58. In general, the most effective means of fire suppression is a(n) _____ attack.
    A. Flanking
    B. Combination
    C. Indirect
    D. Direct

Answer – D
Reference - FFS, p 685

59. What are the two types of fire suppression operations?
    A. Offensive and defensive
    B. Interior and exterior
    C. Rescue and property conservation
    D. Direct and indirect

Answer – A
Reference - FFS, p 680

60. Which special hazard is found on hybrid vehicles?
    A. High-voltage cables
    B. Slow-drain capacitors
    C. Sulfuric acid
    D. Compressed gas cylinders

Answer - A
Reference - FFS, p 697

Chapter 22

61. Which factor must be taken into consideration when fighting a structure fire?
    A. Results of last survey tour
    B. Date of last fire inspection
    C. Length of time the fire has been burning
    D. Building address

Answer - C
Reference - FFS, p

62. As lead of an interior fire crew, you notice a sudden change in fire conditions. After ensuring the safety of your crew. The next thing you should do is:
    A. Order your crew to exit the building
    B. Notify the Incident Commander of changes you observed
    C. Call for personnel accountability report on all interior crews
    D. Contact and give the Safety Officer an update on interior conditions

Answer – B
Reference - FFS, p

63. In order to protect the container from rupture during a flammable gas fire, fire streams should be directed:
    A. Into the involved tank
    B. Around the base of the tank
    C. Onto the tank from a safe distance
    D. To extinguish the fire as soon as possible

Answer – C
Reference - FFS, p 700

Notes on Fire Suppression

Fight fire
  1. Remove fuel (physically), oxygen (smother), or heat (water)
  2. Break chemical chain reaction

Attack strategies
  1. Offensive (interior, go into the building) operations - Room and contents and other small fires, requires more manpower, multiple small handlines, least amount of property damage

246

Fire Suppression

2. Defensive (exterior, surround and drown) operations - Goals is to prevent fire from spreading. Use large handlines and master streams. Used when fire is too large, and risk is too great for fire fighters.

Decisions made by incident commander prior to operations beginning and clearly communicated to personnel. If everyone on a scene does not know what is happening, the IC does not have control of that scene.

Type of attack
1. Direct attack - most effective, straight, or solid stream
2. Indirect attack - when area is ready for flashover, short burst of water applied to ceiling, generates steam which can burn
3. Combination attack - "make circles" to include attack directly on fire and indirectly to ceiling to cool steam, narrow fog pattern. Attack fire then ceiling then fire then ceiling then fire……

Flammable liquids
1. Any type of occupancy
2. Most vehicles involve flammable or combustible liquids
3. Hybrid cars - twelve-volt battery and shut off is typically in the trunk. Larger batteries often under the seat.
4. Two dimensional - spill, pool, or container where only top surface is burning,
5. Three dimensional - burning liquid dripping, spraying, or flowing over the edge of a container. Dry chemical or gas is usually more effective than foam.

Propane
1. Heating, cooking, and vehicle fuels
2. Gas above negative 44F
3. Expansion ratio 270 to 1
4. Containers - space fills with gas above liquid level, piping draws from vapor space, aluminum or steel construction, discharge valve controls flow of gas. Must be in upright position, cylinders equipped with relief valves.
5. Hazards - highly flammable, nontoxic but cause asphyxiation, odorless but hydrogen sulfide added for warning smell, heavier than air

BLEVE - boiling liquid expanding vapor explosion
1. Pressure increases from heat
2. Release valve may open to vent pressure
3. Container may fail violently
4. Prevent with heavy streams of water from a distance.

Flammable gas fire suppression
1. Do not extinguish flames until fuel source is shut off
2. Approach with two 1 ¾ inch lines set on a fog pattern.
3. Team leader is between the lines
4. Once at the tank, reach in and close the valve.
5. Back away from lines that are still flowing.
6. For severe fires, use unattended master streams and evacuate the area.
7. If the relief valve is working, the higher the squeal, the more danger of BLEVE.

Chapter 23
Preincident Planning

1. Which item of preincident plan data is particularly critical for size-up?
   A. Ownership
   B. Access
   C. Lockbox location
   D. Use and occupancy

Answer - D
Reference - FFS, p 717

2. Where is the annunciator panel usually located?
   A. Near the main electrical panel
   B. Near the building entrance
   C. Near the stairway or elevator
   D. Near the sprinkler riser

Answer - B
Reference - FFS, p 718

3. Which document must be provided at an occupancy where a significant volume of hazardous materials is present?
   A. CHEMTREC material reference sheet
   B. Emergency Response Guide
   C. NFPA 49 (Hazardous Chemicals Data)
   D. Material safety data sheet

Answer - D
Reference - FFS, p 725

4. Which type of building construction is also known as heavy timber?
   A. Type I
   B. Type II
   C. Type IV
   D. Type V

Answer - C
Reference - FFS, p 714

Chapter 23

5. Properties that are particularly large or that pose unusual hazards have which type of designation?
    A. Special hazard
    B. Priority location
    C. High risk
    D. Target hazard

Answer - D
Reference - FFS, p 710

6. Which type of building construction is also known as noncombustible?
    A. Type I
    B. Type II
    C. Type IV
    D. Type V

Answer - B
Reference - FFS, p 714

7. Which of the following items is typically included a preincident plan?
    A. Location of occupants
    B. Number of occupants
    C. History of previous incidents
    D. Presence of hazardous materials

Answer - D
Reference - FFS, p 711

8. Fire safety surveys of private residences are:
    A. Required by the NFPA
    B. Voluntary and performed at the request of the homeowner
    C. Required in some jurisdictions
    D. Performed with the primary goal of code compliance

Answer - B
Reference - FFS, p 724

Preincident Planning

9. Why would a low-rise building be equipped with a standpipe system?
    A. To provide pumper support for the sprinkler system
    B. To enable attack lines to be connected near the fire
    C. To reduce water damage
    D. Because of the number of interior partitions

Answer - A
Reference - FFS, p 718

10. If a propane gas or fuel oil tank is present on a property, the preincident plan should indicate the tank's _____.
    A. Capacity
    B. Pipeline diameter
    C. Valve type
    D. Hydro date

Answer - A
Reference - FFS, p 720

11. Which system delivers water from to fire hose outlets on each floor in a high-rise building?
    A. Dry pipe
    B. Standpipe
    C. Water thief
    D. Riser

Answer - B
Reference - FFS, p 718

12. What is the term for a large fire involving multiple structures?
    A. Running fire
    B. Campaign fire
    C. Conflagration
    D. Enfilade

Answer - C
Reference - FFS, p 710

13. Which factor is of particular concern when trying to gain access to a public assembly during an emergency?
    A. Occupants trying to exit
    B. Lack of access routes
    C. Power failure
    D. Security systems

Answer - A
Reference - FFS, p 723

14. Which of the following building features is designed to stop the spread of fire?
    A. Soffit
    B. Purlin
    C. Firewall
    D. Cripple

Answer - C
Reference - FFS, p 187

15. Fire fighters visit a commercial/industrial property to become familiar with a building and anticipate fire behavior during a(n) _____.
    A. Preincident planning survey
    B. Fire inspection
    C. Enforcement survey
    D. Size-up

Answer - A
Reference - FFS, p 710

16. Which of the following is an example of a special hazard?
    A. High-voltage equipment
    B. Healthcare facility
    C. Parking structure
    D. Heavy timber construction

Answer - A
Reference - FFS, p 724

Preincident Planning

17. What is the function of a standpipe system?
    A. Eliminate the need to stretch attack lines from the street level to the fire floor
    B. Provide a means to connect a pumper to a private water system
    C. Provide pumper support to the sprinkler system
    D. Eliminate the need to transport hose to the fire floor

Answer - A
Reference - FFS, p 718

18. For which type of occupancy is a defend-in-place approach to fire protection commonly applied?
    A. Large public assembly venues
    B. Educational facilities
    C. Industrial complexes
    D. Healthcare facilities

Answer - D
Reference - FFS, p 723

19. Which item is of particular concern when preplanning a structure for vertical ventilation?
    A. Multiple ceilings
    B. Blown-in insulation
    C. Hot-mopped roof membrane
    D. HVAC equipment

Answer - A
Reference - FFS, p 722

20. The function of a fire department connection (FDC) is to provide:
    A. The ability to draft without the use of hard suction line
    B. A connection for a pumper to supplement the sprinkler system's water supply
    C. An auxiliary water supply for fire attack
    D. A connection for a pumper into a private water system

Answer - B
Reference - FFS, p 718

Chapter 23

21. A school is an example of a(n) ____ hazard.
    A. Target
    B. High-risk
    C. Elevated
    D. Special

Answer - A
Reference - FFS, p 710

22. Who creates the final preincident plan drawings?
    A. A fire prevention officer
    B. The officer who surveyed the property
    C. A graphic artist
    D. An architect

Answer - B
Reference - FFS, p 710

23. Which of the following is a critical item of information to be included in a preincident plan?
    A. Hydrant locations
    B. Exit path width
    C. Permit record
    D. History of code violations

Answer - A
Reference - FFS, p 711

24. What is a common term for a secure key storage vault mounted on the exterior of a building?
    A. Key code
    B. Key box
    C. Magazine
    D. Lock box

Answer - D
Reference - FFS, p 722

25. What is a common method of storing paper preincident plans?
    A. Three-ring binder
    B. Index card
    C. Loose leaf
    D. Folded, laminated sheet

Answer - A
Reference - FFS, p 710

26. Completed drawings in preincident plans should use _____ symbols.
    A. Architectural
    B. Planometric
    C. Standard
    D. Topographic

Answer - C
Reference - FFS, p 711

27. Which type of building construction is also known as fire resistive?
    A. Type I
    B. Type II
    C. Type IV
    D. Type V

Answer - A
Reference - FFS, p 714

28. Which assumption is made in preincident planning that is not made in fire prevention?
    A. Informed occupants will take responsibility for their safety
    B. A fire will occur
    C. Correction of hazardous conditions will prevent an incident from occurring
    D. Occupants will be unable to help themselves

Answer - B
Reference - FFS, p 710

Chapter 23

29. Which specialized type of fire suppression system is used in areas where flammable liquids are used or stored?
   A. Hydrogenated hydrocarbon
   B. Water mist
   C. Foam
   D. Deluge

Answer - C
Reference - FFS, p 718

30. Which item of information is critical for a private water supply system that feeds both the sprinkler system and the fire hydrants?
   A. The location of the system check valves
   B. The system's ability to simultaneously supply both hydrants and sprinklers
   C. Distance between hydrants and FDCs
   D. The location of the system dry hydrants

Answer - C
Reference - FFS, p 718

31. Which statement about the use of private water-supply systems is correct?
   A. The condition and capacity of the system must be determined prior to use.
   B. These systems are designed to support both sprinkler systems and suppression operations.
   C. These systems are built to the same standards as public systems.
   D. Access to the water supply is typically obtained through drafting hydrants.

Answer - A
Reference - FFS, p 720

32. A high-rise structure is generally defined as being at least _____ in height.
   A. 50 ft (15m)
   B. 75 ft (23m)
   C. 100 ft (30m)
   D. 125 ft (38m)

Answer - B
Reference - FFS, p 723

Preincident Planning

33. Which statement about storing preincident plans on computers is correct?
    A. Paper remains the preferred means of data retrieval in emergency conditions.
    B. The need to make and distribute updated copies is eliminated.
    C. The data are more visible in poor lighting conditions.
    D. Computers are too sensitive for emergency scene conditions.

Answer - B
Reference - FFS, p 711

34. Which hazard poses a greatly increased risk to fire fighters during night operations?
    A. Overhead power lines
    B. Illegal parking
    C. Underground utility vaults
    D. Suspended acoustic ceilings

Answer - A
Reference - FFS, p 720

35. In the absence of any unusual risk factors, preincident plans for one- and two-family residential buildings are:
    A. Simple plot plans
    B. Similar to those prepared for other occupancies
    C. Abbreviated
    D. Not done

Answer - B
Reference - FFS, p 723

36. Which of the following indicates the type and location of the device that has set off the fire alarm in a building?
    A. Monitoring service
    B. Alarm reporting panel
    C. Annunciator panel
    D. Alarm status panel

Answer - C
Reference - FFS, p 1045

37. Which type of building construction is also known as wood frame?
    A. Type I
    B. Type II
    C. Type IV
    D. Type V

Answer - D
Reference - FFS, p 714

38. What is the primary role of a fire alarm system?
    A. Send a signal to the fire department
    B. Send a signal to an alarm monitoring service
    C. Alert occupants to a hazard
    D. Provide occupants with a means of summoning help

Answer – C
Reference - FFS, p 718

39. Which data are of particular relevance in the response phase of an emergency incident?
    A. Construction type
    B. Building access
    C. Built-in protection systems
    D. Occupancy type

Answer - B
Reference - FFS, p

40. Where should a preincident survey begin?
    A. Main entrance
    B. Outside
    C. Lowest floor
    D. Top floor

Answer - B
Reference - FFS, p 711

Preincident Planning

41. To whom should preincident plans be made available?
    A. Command-level staff only
    B. The first-due unit for that location only
    C. Units from the jurisdiction having authority only
    D. Any unit that would respond to an incident at that location

Answer - D
Reference - FFS, p 710

42. For the purpose of a preincident survey, which of the following is a particular concern with underground parking facilities?
    A. Sufficient overhead clearance to permit entry of apparatus
    B. Ability to support the weight of apparatus
    C. Adequacy of natural ventilation
    D. Presence of built-in protection systems

Answer - B
Reference - FFS, p 713

43. Which of the following is a primary factor in calculating the required flow rate for a building?
    A. Age
    B. Water supply
    C. Access
    D. Contents

Answer - D
Reference - FFS, p 718

44. Which statement is correct regarding how a preincident survey should be conducted?
    A. The survey team should be unaccompanied by the property manager/owner.
    B. The survey team should begin the survey at the ground floor interior.
    C. The survey should follow a uniform format.
    D. The survey should be performed after business hours.

Answer – C
Reference - FFS, p 711

Chapter 23

45. An occupancy where there is high potential for loss of life or property from a fire is designated as a(n) hazard.
    A. Special
    B. Extraordinary
    C. Life safety
    D. Target

Answer - D
Reference - FFS, p 710

46. Preincident plans can be useful as aids in _____.
    A. Budget development
    B. Personnel selection
    C. Training activities
    D. Code enforcement

Answer - C
Reference - FFS, p 725

47. A property's surrounding topography is relevant to the response phase of an emergency incident because it _____.
    A. Might render some sides of a building inaccessible
    B. Likely reflects the building layout on the interior
    C. May influence fire behavior
    D. Will influence water runoff

Answer - A
Reference - FFS, p 713

48. Which statement about the use of HVAC equipment in ventilation is correct?
    A. These systems are designed to remove smoke without circulating it around the building.
    B. Instructions for using the system in ventilation should be included on a preincident plan.
    C. The risk of improper use of HVAC for ventilation outweighs the potential benefits.
    D. Power supply to the HVAC system should be shut off and locked out.

Answer - B
Reference - FFS, p 722

Preincident Planning

49. Which of the following is an occupancy subcategory?
    A. Public assembly
    B. Institutional
    C. Commercial
    D. Arena

Answer - D
Reference - FFS, p 717

50. Which NFPA standard contains information on recommended practices for preincident planning?
    A. 1400
    B. 1581
    C. 1600
    D. 1620

Answer - D
Reference - FFS, p 710

51. What is the most challenging aspect of emergency incident operations at a healthcare facility?
    A. Lack of rated partitions
    B. Protection of nonambulatory patients
    C. Pressurized oxygen supplies
    D. Ventilation

Answer – B
Reference - FFS, p 723

52. What is the term for a property that poses a large or unusual risk?
    A. High-risk occupancy
    B. Hazard zone
    C. Threat zone
    D. Target hazard

Answer - D
Reference - FFS, p 710

53. What is an occupancy major use classification?
   A. Commercial
   B. Health care
   C. Educational
   D. Eating/drinking establishment

Answer - A
Reference - FFS, p 717

54. What is the term for a building that is endangered due to an incident in another building?
   A. Liability
   B. Exposure
   C. Endangerment
   D. Risk

Answer - B
Reference - FFS, p 717

55. Ordinary construction is Type _____.
   A. I
   B. II
   C. III
   D. IV

Answer - C
Reference - FFS, p 714

56. A factor in deciding to preplan a structure or area is:
   A. The type of life hazards expected
   B. Buildings with most fire alarms
   C. Only buildings over ten stories in height
   D. Buildings with the most fire violations

Answer - A
Reference - FFS, p 717

57. Accurate diagrams for pre-incident planning are important since:
    A. This form will be used to determine cause and origin of a fire.
    B. They are the basis for fire code violations.
    C. They are used for public fire safety presentations.
    D. This information is used for scene size-up.

Answer - D
Reference - FFS, p 708

Notes on Preincident Planning

NFPA/ISO - Visit all commercial structures annually for preincident planning

ISO class 3 to class 2 - $200 cheaper on insurance

Information gathered during a preincident survey
1. Building location
2. Apparatus access to the exterior of a building
3. Access points to the interior of a building
4. Hydrant locations and alternate water supplies
5. Size of building - dimensions, number of floors
6. Exposures to the fire building and separation distances
7. Type of building construction
8. Building use
9. Type of occupancy - industrial, commercial, residential, assembly, institutional
10. Floor plans
11. Life hazards
12. Exit plans and locations
13. Stairway locations - enclosed or unenclosed
14. Elevator locations and emergency controls
15. Built-in fire protection systems - standpipes and connections, sprinklers and control valves, firewalls
16. Fire detection and alarm systems, fire alarm annunciation panels
17. Utility shut off locations,
18. Ventilation locations
19. Hazardous materials
20. Unusual hazards or concerns
21. Type of incidents expected
22. Sources of potential damage
23. Special resources required
24. General firefighting concerns.

Classification of Buildings
1. Public assembly - theaters, auditoriums, churches, arenas and stadiums, convention centers and meeting halls, bars, and restaurants
2. Institutional - hospitals and nursing homes, schools (school systems usually contract preincident planning for individual schools and make results available to fire departments)
3. Commercial - retail shops, industrial factories, warehouses, parking garages, offices

Occupancy considerations
1. High-rise buildings
2. Assembly occupancies
3. Health care facilities
4. Detention and correctional facilities
5. Residential occupancies

Plan components
1. Detailed diagrams
2. Location and nature of any special hazards
3. Detailed information on the characteristics of a building
4. Additional or special information - special substances (may or may not burn, toxic products), special tools needed

Conducting a preincident survey
1. Conduct with property owner knowledge (appointment, dress professionally)
2. Systematic approach - begin with exterior, move to interior, return visit for large properties
3. Establish most efficient route
4. Confirm street address
5. Note water sources (identify at least two)
6. Identify multiple access points
7. Indicate access blocking barriers
8. What roads lead to the building?
9. Where are the hydrants and fire department connections?
10. Are there security barriers?
11. Are there fire lanes?
12. Are there obstructions limiting access?
13. Can it support the weight of the fire apparatus? Parking garage, bridge
14. Keys or codes required for entry?
15. Natural or topographic features limiting access?
16. Does landscaping or snow prevent access?

17. Is the lock box operational and accessible?
18. Security guards?
19. Is the key holder available?
20. Where is the fire alarm annunciator panel? Is it properly programmed?

Overhead passages and conveyor systems - FedEx is an example of extensive conveyor systems

Remodeled buildings
1. Can remove original fire protection
2. May create new hazards
3. Conduct survey during construction or remodeling
4. Unfinished construction is most vulnerable - cannot limit oxygen or fuel, sprinkler and other fire suppression systems not operational.
5. Uses change over time.

Exposures
1. Other buildings, outside storage
2. Survey - construction, fire load, distance, ease of ignition

Automatic sprinkler system
1. System presence and area covered
2. Interior or exterior water control valves
3. Record location of nearby water supply
4. Note area served by fire department connection.

Special fire extinguishing systems - airports
Note water required if building is 25%, 50%, or 75% involved.

Preincident plans for search and rescue
1. Day and night occupancy
2. Note places for ladder placement
3. List overhead obstructions.
4. Commercial structures usually have power and telephone underground

Ventilation
1. Roof types - Wood covered by tar and covered by gravel, wood covered by tar, metal sheeting

Healthcare facilities
1. Greatest challenge is protecting non-ambulatory patients
2. Defend in place - often insufficient staff for patients that need escape assistance

3. Horizontal evacuation - move patients to safer area on the same floor

Detention and Correctional Facilities
1. Move inmates while protecting firefighters
2. Security practices may affect access to building and occupancy areas.

Residential occupancies
1. Most plans cover multifamily residences
2. General neighborhood surveys are informative
3. Homeowners may request

Chapter 24
Fire and Emergency Medical Care

1. Keeping EMS providers updated on changes in the field is the function of _____.
    A. A continuous quality improvement program
    B. The national registry process
    C. Treatment protocols and procedures
    D. Continuing medical education classes

Answer - D
Reference - FFS, p 737

2. Through which organization are Emergency Medical Responders nationally registered?
    A. National Registry of Emergency Medical Technicians
    B. U.S. Department of Health and Human Services
    C. FEMA
    D. International Red Cross

Answer - A
Reference - FFS, p 735

3. What is the best perspective to maintain when treating a patient?
    A. Your duty is to do what is right for the patient regardless of any objection on that person's part
    B. Treat the patient as you would want to be treated if you were in his or her position
    C. Your obligation to the community comes before your obligation to the patient
    D. You must accept that there are some situations where you will be powerless to help

Answer - B
Reference - FFS, p 738

4. Approximately _____ percent of fire departments in the United States provide patient transportation services.
    A. 35
    B. 45
    C. 55
    D. 65

Answer - C
Reference - FFS, p 732

Chapter 24

5. What is the lowest level of training qualified to perform BLS skills?
    A. Emergency Medical Responder
    B. Advanced first aid
    C. Emergency Medical Technician
    D. First responder

Answer - A
Reference - FFS, p 734

6. Which of the following is an Emergency Medical Responder (EMR) skill?
    A. Administration of oxygen
    B. Use of an AED
    C. Attending patients during ambulance transport
    D. Use of airway adjuncts

Answer - B
Reference - FFS, p 734

7. Advanced life support personnel operate as the extension of:
    A. The agency
    B. The public health system
    C. A physician
    D. The first responders

Answer - C
Reference - FFS, p 734

8. In general, which type of EMS delivery has been found to provide the highest quality of care?
    A. It varies by community
    B. Fire department EMS
    C. Separate EMS agency
    D. Combination

Answer - A
Reference - FFS, p 737

Fire and Emergency Medical Care

9. Fire fighters should regard the citizens of their community as:
   A. Taxpayers
   B. Clients
   C. Consumers
   D. Customers

Answer - A
Reference - FFS, p 733

10. Which agency establishes the national curriculum standards for EMS courses?
    A. National Fire Protection Association (NFPA)
    B. Department of Health and Human Services (HHS)
    C. Department of Transportation (DOT)
    D. Federal Emergency Management Agency (FEMA)

Answer - C
Reference - FFS, p 734

11. What is the minimum level of training necessary to provide care to a victim in an ambulance?
    A. First responder
    B. EMT
    C. EMR
    D. Paramedic

Answer - B
Reference - FFS, p 735

12. What is an occlusive dressing used for?
    A. Preventing infection
    B. Stopping bleeding
    C. Treating burns
    D. Sealing chest wounds

Answer - D
Reference - FFS, p

Chapter 24

13. With which group would discussion of confidential patient information be acceptable?
    A. Friends and neighbors of the patient
    B. Other EMS or fire personnel not involved in patient care
    C. EMS crews from another shift
    D. None of the above

Answer - D
Reference - FFS, p 740

14. Each EMS system has a medical director with _____ credentials.
    A. Critical care nurse
    B. Physician
    C. EMT-paramedic
    D. EMS administrator

Answer - B
Reference - FFS, p 738

15. Which item is required for EMS provider recertification?
    A. Continuing medical education (CME)
    B. A specified minimum number of patient contacts
    C. Clinical experience hours
    D. Continuous service hours

Answer - A
Reference - FFS, p 737

16. Approximately ____ percent of U.S. fire departments provide some level of EMS to their communities.
    A. 65
    B. 75
    C. 85
    D. 95

Answer - D
Reference - FFS, p 732

Fire and Emergency Medical Care

17. Which of the following is exclusively a paramedic-level skill?
    A. Administering medications
    B. Ambulance operation
    C. Extrication
    D. Use of an AED

Answer - A
Reference - FFS, p 735

18. What is the defining characteristic of a fire department EMS system?
    A. Delivery of ALS-level care
    B. Provision of both medical and transport services
    C. Provision of first-tier medical response
    D. Training of all personnel to a specified level

Answer - B
Reference - FFS, p 737

19. What is a disadvantage of combination fire department/EMS systems?
    A. A fire company may be out of service for a long time while waiting for an ambulance
    B. Fire company personnel are utilized for patient transport
    C. Responsibility for patient care is delegated to less qualified personnel
    D. Fire department personnel provide a lower level of care

Answer - A
Reference - FFS, p 737

20. Which of the following is exclusively a Paramedic-level skill?
    A. Automated defibrillation
    B. Treating shock
    C. Moving trauma victims
    D. Monitoring heart rhythms

Answer - D
Reference - FFS, p 735

Chapter 24

21. Emergency medical services are provided at two levels. What is one of those?
    A. Basic first aid
    B. First responder
    C. Basic life support
    D. Advanced first aid

Answer - C
Reference - FFS, p 734

22. Which acronym refers to a level of emergency medical service provision?
    A. EOA
    B. ALS
    C. FSTC
    D. ASUR

Answer – B. Advanced Life Support
Reference - FFS, p 735

23. In a fire department EMS system, at which level of training are the first response and transport services provided?
    A. Both are ALS
    B. First response is ALS and transport is BLS
    C. First response is BLS and transport is ALS
    D. Either one can be BLS or ALS

Answer - D
Reference - FFS, p 737

24. Which level of EMS service delivery consists primarily of patient assessment, oxygen delivery, and moving/lifting of patients?
    A. Basic life support
    B. Transitional life support
    C. Intermediate life support
    D. Advanced life support

Answer - A
Reference - FFS, p 734

25. What is an advantage of having the medical first response provided by the fire department?
    A. Reduced wait times for patient transport
    B. Fewer personnel required to provide care
    C. Access to additional funding resources
    D. Immediate care is available for injured fire fighters

Answer - A
Reference - FFS, p 737

26. Who usually decides which agencies will provide EMS?
    A. Elected officials
    B. The Local Emergency Planning Committee (LEPC)
    C. The chief fire official
    D. An accreditation committee

Answer - A
Reference - FFS, p 737

27. HIPAA applies specifically to:
    A. EMS providers
    B. healthcare providers
    C. certified or registered medical personnel
    D. "covered entities"

Answer - D
Reference - FFS, p 740

28. Who serves as liaison between the medical community, hospitals, and the EMS providers?
    A. Local department of health designee
    B. Medical director
    C. Regional EMS program coordinator
    D. Agency EMS program coordinator

Answer - B
Reference - FFS, p 739

Chapter 24

29. An EMS system where the fire department provides medical first response and another agency provides patient transportation is a _____ system.
    A. Combination
    B. Tiered
    C. Contract
    D. Split

Answer - A
Reference - FFS, p 737

30. What is an example of indirect medical control?
    A. Phone/radio contact
    B. Continuing medical education
    C. Standing orders
    D. Combination EMS system

Answer - C
Reference - FFS, p 739

31. Administering intravenous fluids and medications are skills performed by a fire fighter trained to the _____ level.
    A. Basic life support
    B. Transitional life support
    C. Intermediate life support
    D. Advanced life support

Answer - D
Reference - FFS, p 735

32. Who provides online medical control?
    A. An EMS physician
    B. An EMT-Paramedic
    C. The company officer
    D. The most qualified responder

Answer - A
Reference - FFS, p 734

33. An Emergency Medical Technician training course is a minimum of _____ hours.
   A. 60
   B. 80
   C. 110
   D. 150

Answer – C
Reference - FFS, p 735

34. How long is the typical Emergency Medical Responder (EMR) course?
   A. 16 hours
   B. 24 hours
   C. 30 hours
   D. 40 hours or more

Answer – D. For example, the course with the American Red Cross is 56 hours.
Reference - FFS, p 734

35. Which level of training is designed specifically for people such as police officers, teachers, and daycare providers who encounter medical emergencies as part of their jobs?
   A. Emergency Medical Responder
   B. Emergency Medical Technician
   C. EMT-Intermediate
   D. Standard first aid

Answer – A
Reference - FFS, p 734

Chapter 25
Emergency Medical Care

1. Where does gas exchange occur?
   A. Meninges
   B. Pulmonary arteries
   C. Bronchioles
   D. Alveoli

Answer - D
Reference - FFS, p

2. What prevents food or water from entering the trachea?
   A. Epiglottis
   B. Tympanum
   C. Vallecula
   D. Arytenoid cartilage

Answer - A
Reference - FFS, p

3. How is hepatitis B spread?
   A. Contact with infected blood
   B. Contact with airborne particles
   C. Intimate sexual contact
   D. Contact with urine or feces
   E. A and C

Answer - E
Reference - FFS, p

4. What is the medical term for the windpipe?
   A. Trachea
   B. Larynx
   C. Esophagus
   D. Epiglottis

Answer - A
Reference - FFS, p

5. Which part of the circulatory system carries blood to the heart?
    A. Arteries
    B. Veins
    C. Arterioles
    D. Capillaries

Answer - B
Reference - FFS, p

6. Which NFPA standard contains information on a fire department infection control program?
    A. 1500
    B. 1521
    C. 1581
    D. 1701

Answer – C
Reference – FFS, p

7. Which part of the body is especially prone to turning pale or blue as a result of inadequate breathing?
    A. Underside of the wrists
    B. Sclera
    C. Lips
    D. Ears

Answer - B
Reference - FFS, p

8. What is the dome-shaped muscle between the chest and the abdomen?
    A. Diaphragm
    B. Peritoneum
    C. Abdominal fascia
    D. Omentum

Answer - A
Reference - FFS, p

9. For how long should you check the carotid pulse of an unconscious adult?
    A. 3 to 5 seconds
    B. 5 to 10 seconds
    C. 10 to 15 seconds
    D. 15 to 20 seconds

Answer - B
Reference - FFS, p

10, What should rescuers do if they hear a cracking sound while performing CPR?
    A. Decrease compression depth slightly
    B. Nothing; continue compressions
    C. Decompress the abdomen
    D. Check and correct hand position

Answer - D
Reference - FFS, p

11. What is the most serious type of bleeding?
    A. Arterial
    B. Venous
    C. Capillary
    D. Alveolar

Answer - A
Reference - FFS, p

12. Which technique is used to assist a conscious infant with a severe airway obstruction?
    A. Both back slaps and chest thrusts
    B. Back slaps
    C. Chest thrusts
    D. Abdominal thrusts

Answer - A
Reference - FFS, p

Emergency Medical Care

13. What is the most common cause of shock?
    A. Psychological trauma
    B. Heart attack
    C. Fluid loss
    D. Allergic reaction

Answer - C
Reference - FFS, p 788

14. For infant CPR, which pulse is checked?
    A. Brachial
    B. Carotid
    C. Radial
    D. Pedal

Answer - A
Reference - FFS, p

15. Which sound is a common indication that the tongue of an unconscious victim is obstructing the airway?
    A. Wheezing
    B. Gurgling
    C. Snoring
    D. Whistling

Answer - C
Reference - FFS, p

16. What is the initial treatment for a chemical burn?
    A. Flush the contaminated area
    B. Brush the material off the victim
    C. Apply a sterile dressing
    D. Administer oxygen

Answer - A
Reference - FFS, p

Chapter 25

17. A rapid, weak pulse is most commonly associated with:
    A. Respiratory difficulty
    B. Shock
    C. Stroke
    D. Allergic reaction

Answer - C
Reference - FFS, p

18. The set of measures recommended by the CDC to prevent exposure to blood and bodily fluids of victims are known as _____.
    A. Standard precautions
    B. Body substance isolation
    C. Universal precautions
    D. Body fluid isolation

Answer - A
Reference - FFS, p 748

19. Gastric distention increases the likelihood that the victim will:
    A. Vomit
    B. Insist on sitting up
    C. Stop breathing
    D. Arrest

Answer - A
Reference - FFS, p

20. How does the use of a pressure point control bleeding?
    A. A nerve is tricked into constricting an artery
    B. A fluid dam is created in the soft tissue
    C. A major blood vessel is compressed against a bone
    D. Clotting factors are held in place

Answer - C
Reference - FFS, p

Emergency Medical Care

21. During rescue breathing, what should be done with firmly attached dental appliances?
   A. Nothing
   B. They should be removed if gentle pressure alone is sufficient to detach them
   C. They should be removed
   D. Single or double bridges should be left in place; all other dental appliances should be removed

Answer - A
Reference - FFS, p

22. How is tuberculosis spread?
   A. Through the use of contaminated needles
   B. Through the air when an infected person coughs or sneezes
   C. Through contact with infected saliva
   D. Through intimate sexual contact only

Answer - B
Reference - FFS, p

23. In an average adult, the loss of as little as _____ of blood may cause shock.
   A. 1 pint (0.5 L)
   B. 2 pints (1 L)
   C. 3 pints (1.5L)
   D. 4 pints (2L)

Answer – B
Reference – FFS, p 788

24. Brain cells begin dying after _____ minutes without oxygen.
   A. 2-4
   B. 4-6
   C. 6-8
   D. 8-10

Answer - B
Reference - FFS, p

25. How can arterial bleeding be recognized?
    A. It spurts from the wound
    B. It is dark red
    C. It oozes steadily from the wound
    D. It is accompanied by serous fluid

Answer - A
Reference - FFS, p

26. When performing an abdominal thrust, where does the fire fighter place the thumb side of the fist?
    A. On the belly button
    B. Below the belly button
    C. On the sternum
    D. Midway between the belly button and the xiphoid

Answer - D
Reference - FFS, p

27. What is the most common cause of total lack of respirations in adults?
    A. Choking
    B. Heart attack
    C. Drowning
    D. Trauma

Answer - A
Reference - FFS, p

28. What occurs when air is forced into the stomach instead of the lungs during rescue breathing?
    A. Cardiac tamponade
    B. Gastric distention
    C. Aspiration pneumonia
    D. Subcutaneous emphysema

Answer - B
Reference - FFS, p

29. What is the first step when treating an electrical burn victim?
   A. Cool the burned area
   B. Assess the level of consciousness
   C. Determine whether the victim is still in contact with the electrical source
   D. Open the airway

Answer - C
Reference - FFS, p

30. What is the major artery in the neck?
   A. Radial
   B. Brachial
   C. Carotid
   D. Femoral

Answer - C
Reference - FFS, p

31. Which piece of protective equipment is of particular importance when caring for a victim with a cough?
   A. Surgical mask
   B. Gown
   C. Goggles
   D. HEPA respirator

Answer - A
Reference - FFS, p

32. Which type of bleeding is characterized by a steady flow of dark red blood?
   A. Venous
   B. Arterial
   C. Serous
   D. Capillary

Answer – A
Reference - FFS, p

33. What is the correct procedure when a victim regurgitates during CPR?
    A. Roll the victim on his or her side and clear the vomit
    B. Suction the oropharynx between ventilations
    C. Continue CPR without interruption
    D. Increase the ventilation pressure

Answer - A
Reference - FFS, p

34. Which type of shock is caused by a severe allergic reaction to a foreign substance?
    A. Septic
    B. Anaphylactic
    C. Neurogenic
    D. Allergenic

Answer - B
Reference - FFS, p

35. What is the most common cause of cardiac arrest in children?
    A. Cardiac myopathy
    B. A breathing problem
    C. Meningitis
    D. A congenital defect

Answer - B
Reference - FFS, p

36. What is the treatment for a severe airway obstruction?
    A. The jaw-thrust technique
    B. The Heimlich maneuvers
    C. Insertion of a rescue airway
    D. Back blows

Answer - B
Reference - FFS, p

37. After rescuers have checked and corrected a victim's airway, what should they check and correct next?
    A. Level of consciousness
    B. Circulation
    C. Breathing
    D. Bleeding

Answer - C
Reference - FFS, p

38. What is the pressure wave generated by the pumping action of the heart?
    A. Diastole
    B. The pulse
    C. Blood pressure
    D. Peristalsis

Answer - B
Reference - FFS, p

39. Which cells are the most sensitive to oxygen deprivation?
    A. Brain
    B. Liver
    C. Skin
    D. Heart

Answer - A
Reference - FFS, p

40. What is the relationship between HIV and AIDS?
    A. HIV and AIDS are two different diseases entirely
    B. The relationship between the two has not been established
    C. AIDS is the virus that causes HIV
    D. HIV is the virus that causes AIDS

Answer - D
Reference - FFS, p

41. What is the correct initial treatment for a chemical burn of the eye?
    A. Cover the eye with moist sterile gauze and transport without delay
    B. Flush the eye with water for 5 minutes
    C. Flush the eye with water for 10 minutes
    D. Flush the eye with water for 20 minutes

Answer - D
Reference - FFS, p

42. What does the medical term "shock" mean?
    A. Failure of the circulatory system
    B. A sudden overwhelming emotional reaction
    C. A severe systemic infection
    D. Failure of the nervous system

Answer - A
Reference - FFS, p

43. Which body substance is a common transmitter of HIV?
    A. Saliva
    B. Tears
    C. Urine
    D. Vaginal secretions

Answer - D
Reference - FFS, p

44. What is the most common source of airway obstruction?
    A. Food
    B. A nonfood object
    C. Vomitus
    D. The tongue

Answer - D
Reference - FFS, p

45. What is the major artery in the groin?
    A. Femoral
    B. Inguinal
    C. Iliac
    D. Tibial

Answer - B
Reference - FFS, p 772

46. What is a function of the circulatory system?
    A. Transport oxygenated blood to the lungs
    B. Absorb oxygen from body tissues
    C. Transport carbon dioxide to the lungs
    D. Absorb carbon dioxide from the alveoli

Answer - C
Reference - FFS, p

47. In two-rescuer CPR on an infant, compressions should be performed with the:
    A. Two thumbs/encircling hands technique
    B. Ring and middle fingers
    C. Ring, middle, and index fingers
    D. Heel of one hand

Answer - A
Reference - FFS, p

48. What is the major artery in the arm?
    A. Humeral
    B. Subclavian
    C. Radial
    D. Brachial

Answer - D
Reference - FFS, p 772

49. Which emotional problem accounts for twenty percent of violent attacks?
    A. Depression
    B. Hyperactivity disorder
    C. Attachment disorder
    D. Autism

Answer - A
Reference - FFS, p 802

50. What is a cause of shock by pump failure?
    A. Systemic infection
    B. Spinal injury
    C. Vasodilation
    D. Heart attack

Answer - D
Reference - FFS, p 788

51. Which CDC policy is based on the assumption that all victims are potential carriers of bloodborne pathogens?
    A. Standard precautions
    B. Universal precautions
    C. Exposure control
    D. Pathogen control

Answer - A
    Reference - FFS, p

52. Which function do red blood cells perform?
    A. Provide energy for metabolism
    B. Form clots
    C. Transport oxygen
    D. Fight infection

Answer - C
Reference - FFS, p

53. Which is the most serious hazard for a rescuer performing mouth-to-mouth rescue breathing?
    A. Gastric distention
    B. Aspiration
    C. Exposure to pathogens
    D. Vomiting

Answer - C
Reference - FFS, p

54. What is the tube though which food passes?
    A. Trachea
    B. Carina
    C. Esophagus
    D. Larynx

Answer - C
Reference - FFS, p

55. Which type of bleeding is characterized by the blood oozing out?
    A. Venous
    B. Arterial
    C. Internal
    D. Capillary

Answer - D
Reference - FFS, p

56. Which of the following is part of the management of shock?
    A. Place the victim in a sitting position
    B. Elevate the victim's legs
    C. Provide fluid replacement by mouth
    D. Keep the victim cool

Answer - B
Reference - FFS, p

Chapter 25

57. Blood that leaves the right ventricle is pumped directly to the:
    A. Lungs
    B. Left ventricle
    C. Right atrium
    D. Aorta

Answer – A. The right ventricle receives blood from the right atrium and pumps blood into the pulmonary artery and then to the lungs.
Reference - FFS, p

58. HIV, HBV, and HCV are:
    A. chemical warfare agents
    B. carcinogens
    C. blood clotting factors
    D. bloodborne pathogens

Answer - D
Reference - FFS, p

59. What is the first step in assessing a victim's airway?
    A. Attempt to give two full breaths
    B. Check the victim's level of responsiveness
    C. Perform the jaw-thrust technique
    D. Lift up and forward on the chin

Answer - B
Reference - FFS, p

60. Which is a correct statement about victim vomiting during CPR?
    A. It is a sign of effective CPR.
    B. It is usually a result of incorrectly performed compressions.
    C. It is a common occurrence.
    D. If it happens, CPR should continue without interruption.

Answer - B
Reference - FFS, p

61. In which situation would you raise the legs of a victim in shock?
    A. Spine injury
    B. Head injury
    C. Leg injury
    D. Arm injury

Answer - C
Reference - FFS, p

62. What is a closed wound?
    A. Abrasion
    B. Bruise
    C. Laceration
    D. Puncture

Answer - B
Reference - FFS, p

63. What is placed directly on a wound to control bleeding and prevent further contamination?
    A. Tourniquet
    B. Bandage
    C. Dressing
    D. Splint

Answer - C
Reference - FFS, p

64. What is the second step to take in controlling external bleeding?
    A. Direct pressure
    B. Pressure points
    C. Tourniquet
    D. Elevation

Answer - D
Reference - FFS, p

Chapter 25

65. Who determines the required immunizations for fire fighters?
    A. Local health officer
    B. CDC
    C. Personal doctor
    D. Agency medical director

Answer - D
Reference - FFS, p

66. The correct rate of chest compressions for adult CPR is _____ compressions per minute:
    A. 60
    B. 80
    C. 100
    D. 120

Answer - C
Reference - FFS, p

67. What is the purpose of the head tilt—chin lift technique?
    A. Examine the pharynx
    B. Open the airway
    C. Protect the spine
    D. Feel the carotid pulse

Answer - B
Reference - FFS, p

68. What is the term for discoloration of the parts of a deceased person's body closest to the ground?
    A. Morbid coagulation
    B. Chromatis mortis
    C. Myasthenia gravis
    D. Dependent lividity

Answer – D
Reference - FFS, p

69. Which type of burn is also known as a third-degree burn?
    A. Full-thickness burn
    B. Chemical burn
    C. Superficial burn
    D. Partial-thickness burn

Answer - A
Reference - FFS, p

70. What are the tiny air sacs at the end of an airway called?
    A. Alveoli
    B. Pulmonary capillaries
    C. Mediastia
    D. Bronchioles

Answer – A
Reference - FFS, p

71. What is the term for a heart that is not contracting?
    A. Shock
    B. Stroke
    C. Cardiac arrest
    D. Heart attack

Answer - C
Reference - FFS, p

72. What is the most critical sign of inadequate breathing?
    A. Absence of chest movement
    B. Retractions
    C. Wheezing
    D. Pale or blue skin color

Answer - A
Reference - FFS, p

Chapter 25

73. What is the ratio of chest compressions to ventilations in one-rescuer adult CPR?
    A. 15:1
    B. 30:2
    C. 15:2

Answer - B
Reference - FFS, p

74. Microorganisms capable of causing disease are called:
    A. Septogens
    B. Pathogens
    C. Contagion
    D. Microbes

Answer - B
Reference - FFS, p

75. What is the legal term for discontinuing CPR without either the order of a physician or hand-off of the victim to someone of equal or superior training?
    A. Abandonment
    B. Nonfeasance
    C. Negligence
    D. Dereliction

Answer – A
Reference - FFS, p

Chapter 26
Vehicle Rescue and Extrication

1. What must occur before the ram or high-lift jack can be removed in a dash displacement?
   A. The victim must be removed from the vehicle
   B. The roof must be removed
   C. Cribbing must be built to support the sill
   D. The seat must be displaced rearward

Answer – C
Reference - FFS, p 831

2. A vehicle air bag will remain energized until the:
   A. Airbag capacitor is fully discharged
   B. Battery is disconnected
   C. Ignition key is removed
   D. Safety switch is flipped

Answer – B
Reference - FFS, p

3. A windshield is made of _____ glass.:
   A. Laminated
   B. Dichroic
   C. Tempered
   D. Composite

Answer – A
Reference - FFS, p 824

4. How can a vehicle powered by compressed natural gas (CNG) be identified?
   A. A small CNG decal on the lower corner of the passenger-side windshield
   B. The gas cylinder will be visible between the rear axle and bumper
   C. A high-pressure filling coupling in place of the gasoline fill spout
   D. CNG stickers on the front and back of the vehicle

Answer – D
Reference - FFS, p 810

5. What is the correct tool for removing a windshield?
   A. Axe
   B. Spring-loaded center punch
   C. Rotary saw
   D. Air chisel

Answer – A
Reference - FFS, p 829

6. Where should plywood be placed with rescue-lift air bags?
   A. Between the bag and the ground
   B. Between stacked bags
   C. Between the bag and the load
   D. None of the above

Answer – A
Reference - FFS, p 821

7. When doing a dash displacement, which tool is used to push the dash forward?
   A. Ratcheting strut
   B. Rescue-lift air bag
   C. Hydraulic ram
   D. Come along

Answer – C
Reference - FFS, p 832

8. Which statement about gaining access through a windshield is correct?
   A. The windshield is easily shattered with a spring-loaded punch.
   B. The windshield is the entry point of choice for access to front-seat passengers.
   C. Windshield removal is a quick and easy operation.
   D. There are usually easier ways to gain access.

Answer – D
Reference - FFS, p 829

9. What is the first step in deactivating an air bag?
   A. Flip the safety switch in the glove compartment
   B. Cut the orange wires in the rocker panel
   C. Disconnect the sensor unit
   D. Disconnect the battery

Answer – D
Reference - FFS, p

10. How are traffic hazards best managed?
    A. Road closure
    B. By law enforcement personnel
    C. Strategic placement of apparatus
    D. Use of cones and flares

Answer – B
Reference - FFS, p 816

11. What is used to prevent the dash from moving back after it has been displaced?
    A. Hydraulic ram
    B. Jack
    C. Cribbing
    D. Spreaders

Answer – C
Reference - FFS, p 832

12. What should be done if there is a small gap between the top of a box crib and the object being raised?
    A. Close the gap with wooden wedges
    B. Carefully lower the object onto the top of the stack
    C. Move the stack to a location where it fits snugly
    D. Use an air bag to fill the gap

Answer – A
Reference - FFS, p 818

Chapter 26

13. Which alternative fuel is often used in buses and delivery vans?
    A. Compressed natural gas
    B. Methanol
    C. Propane
    D. Liquefied petroleum gas

Answer – A
Reference - FFS, p 810

14. Which tool is best suited for breaking tempered glass?
    A. Glass saw
    B. Axe blade
    C. Maul
    D. Spring-loaded punch

Answer – D
Reference - FFS, p 824

15. What is the term for a vehicle that operates using a battery-powered electric motor combined with a conventional gasoline engine?
    A. Hybrid
    B. Alternative fuel
    C. Electric
    D. Fuel cell

Answer – A
Reference - FFS, p 811

16. If normal methods of moving a seat backward do not work, what is the next technique to attempt?
    A. Roof removal
    B. Cutting the seat mounts
    C. Dash displacement
    D. "B" post removal

Answer – B
Reference - FFS, p 828

17. What is the most efficient and widely used tool used to open a jammed vehicle door?
    A. Pry axe
    B. Come along
    C. Rabbet tool
    D. Hydraulic spreader

Answer – A
Reference - FFS, p 826

18. What is the minimum size of hose line for fire protection at a vehicle accident?
    A. Booster
    B. 1" (25 mm)
    C. 1 ½" (38 mm)
    D. 1 ¾" (45 mm)

Answer – C
Reference - FFS, p 817

19. What is the first step in a dash displacement?
    A. Secure or remove the front doors
    B. Put a relief cut in the "A" post
    C. Wrap the steering column
    D. Notch the "B" post

Answer – A
Reference - FFS, p 830

20. What is the designation for the posts located between the front and rear doors on a four-door vehicle?
    A. The "2" posts
    B. The "B" posts
    C. The mid-posts
    D. The short posts

Answer – B
Reference - FFS, p 811

Chapter 26

21. Which type of rescue-lift air bag is most commonly used by fire fighters?
    A. High pressure
    B. Type 11
    C. High lift
    D. Medium pressure

Answer – A
Reference - FFS, p 821

22. When removing the victim from the vehicle, who directs the move?
    A. The company officer
    B. The most qualified medical provider
    C. The person holding the victim's c-spine
    D. The person at the foot of the backboard

Answer – C
Reference - FFS, p 833

23. If the air bag did not deploy during a vehicle accident, what must be done prior to disentangling a victim?
    A. Place a short back board between the victim and the steering wheel
    B. Puncture the air bag
    C. Cut the steering column
    D. Disconnect the battery

Answer – D
Reference - FFS, p

24. Vehicle air bags may remain energized for as long as _____ minutes after the vehicle battery has been disconnected.
    A. 0
    B. 5
    C. 10
    D. It varies with the manufacturer

Answer – D
Reference - FFS, p

Vehicle Rescue and Extrication

25. After step chocks are placed under the side of the vehicle, rescuers may:
    A. Pull the valve stems from the tires
    B. Remove the box crib
    C. Chock the wheels
    D. Set the parking brake

Answer – C
Reference - FFS, p 818

26. What is laminated glass?
    A. A single sheet of plastic sandwiched between two sheets of glass
    B. A sheet of tempered glass encased in a plastic film
    C. A single sheet of glass sandwiched between two sheets of plastic
    D. A layer of tempered glass bonded to a layer of acrylic

Answer – A
Reference - FFS, p 829, 1141

27. Which type of glass is the rear window of a vehicle?
    A. Laminated
    B. Dichroic
    C. Tempered
    D. Composite

Answer – C
Reference - FFS, p 824

28. What is the designation for the posts located behind the rear doors or rear passenger compartment windows?
    A. The rear posts
    B. The "3" posts
    C. The "C" posts
    D. The long posts

Answer – C
Reference - FFS, p 811

Chapter 26

29. Where should the posts be cut when removing the roof of a vehicle?
    A. Between the hinges
    B. As low as possible
    C. At the junction with the roof
    D. At the level of the windowsill

Answer – B
Reference - FFS, p 831

30. What is the correct procedure when performing extrication in a vehicle with an undeployed air bag?
    A. Place a rigid barrier between the victim and the air bag
    B. Stay away from the front of the air bag
    C. Cut the orange wires in the rocker panel
    D. Remove the steering wheel

Answer – C
Reference - FFS, p

31. What divides the engine compartment of a car from the passenger compartment?
    A. "A" wall
    B. Dashboard
    C. Firewall
    D. Partition

Answer – C
Reference - FFS, p 811

32. What are step chocks commonly used for?
    A. Stabilize a vehicle's suspension
    B. Support the sill during a dash roll-up
    C. Prevent a vehicle from rolling
    D. Create a fulcrum

Answer – A
Reference - FFS, p 818

33. How are most windshields affixed in place?
    A. Spring retention clips
    B. Plastic glue
    C. Mastic
    D. A rubber loop gasket

Answer – B
Reference - FFS, p 829

34. What is the most common technique for gaining access to a vehicle after a collision?
    A. Roof removal
    B. Back or side glass removal
    C. Door displacement
    D. Windshield removal

Answer – C
Reference - FFS, p 825

35. What is the voltage of the electrical system on most conventional vehicles?
    A. 6 volts
    B. 12 volts
    C. 24 volts
    D. 36 volts

Answer – B
Reference - FFS, p 810

36. What is the designation for the posts closest to the front on a car?
    A. "A" posts
    B. Forward posts
    C. Bow posts
    D. "I" posts

Answer – A
Reference - FFS, p 811

37. Which of the following is a correct rescue-lift air bag safety principle?
    A. Bags must rest on the ground during inflation
    B. When bags are stacked, inflate the top bag first
    C. Separate stacked bags with a section of plywood
    D. Lift an inch, crib an inch

Answer – D
Reference - FFS, p 818

38. Which hazard is unique to CNG- and LPG-powered vehicle fires?
    A. Potential for three-dimensional fire
    B. Slow-drain capacitors
    C. Highly toxic products of combustion
    D. BLEVE

Answer – D
Reference - FFS, p 810

39. What is the last part of a windshield that should be cut?
    A. The most accessible part
    B. The side
    C. The bottom
    D. The top

Answer – C
Reference - FFS, p 829

40. What is another term for the firewall of a vehicle?
    A. Dashboard
    B. Partition
    C. Firestop
    D. Bulkhead

Answer – D
Reference - FFS, p 811

Vehicle Rescue and Extrication

41. The primary hazard for firefighters during a vehicle extrication is:
    A. Traffic
    B. Electrical
    C. Bloodborne pathogens
    D. Fire

Answer – A
Reference - FFS, p 814

42. Which is a method to identify a vehicle supplied by compressed natural gas?
    A. A placard on the front/rear bumper
    B. The cylinder is visible in the back seat
    C. The firefighter will be able to smell the gas as they approach the vehicle
    D. All states require a sticker on the front windshield

Answer – A
Reference - FFS, p 812

45. To chock the wheels of a vehicle involved in an accident, the firefighter should:
    A. Use hydraulic chocks that will automatically adjust to any potential vehicle movement
    B. Chock the wheels on the uphill side
    C. Use stabilizing jacks and airbags to ensure the vehicle will not move
    D. Chock the wheels in both directions

Answer – D
Reference - FFS, p 819

46. When using a spring-loaded center punch to open a window, the firefighter should press the center punch at the:
    A. Center of the window
    B. Upper corner of the window
    C. At the top of the window
    D. Lower corner of the window

Answer – D
Reference - FFS, p 824

Chapter 26

47. What difference does a hybrid vehicle have compared to a conventional gasoline powered vehicle?
    A. Diesel
    B. Compressed nature gas (CNG)
    C. High voltage
    D. Hydraulic

Answer – C
Reference - FFS, p 811

48. When using rescue lift airbags, boards, and plywood must not be used:
    A. Between or above them
    B. Underneath them
    C. On either side of them
    D. Anywhere within fifteen feet of them

Answer – A
Reference - FFS, p 821

Notes on Vehicle Extrication

Frame
1. Provides attachment points
2. Unibody in most modern cars, lighter weight vehicles, sometimes trucks

Traffic hazards and arrival
1. Secure scene - use large emergency vehicles to block approaching motorists, angle towards traffic to deflect oncoming vehicles if possible
2. Place traffic cones or flares
3. Firefighters must be visible and alert - traffic vest and/or bunker gear
4. Hazards - spilled fuels, presence of fire, downed or damaged power line, (call power company) compressed gas cylinders
5. Have water extinguisher and if entrapment, charged hand line available

Other hazards
1. Weather - rain, sleet, ice, snow
2. HAZMAT
3. Infectious body fluids
4. Sharp edges and objects
5. Violent behavior by vehicle occupants
6. Family pets

Vehicle Rescue and Extrication

Cribbing
1. Stabilize car
2. Length of wood to prevent a vehicle from moving forward or backward
3. Step chocks - lift car and slide underneath
4. Box cribs - cribbing stacked at right angles. 4x4 cribbing has a 6000 lb. weight rating per contact point. It can therefore hold 24,000 lbs. (12 tons), also 3x3 and 2x2 configurations. Can also use for structure collapse. Use airbag to lift car.
5. Wedges - used to snug up loose cribbing or when using airbags, same width as cribbing.

Rescue lift air bags
1. Life a vehicle or object off a victim
2. Low pressure (5-20 psi) airbags - recovery, vehicle rescue, moves feet
3. High pressure (90-110 psi) - vulcanized rubber with steel reinforcement, Moves inches

Access to the victim
1. Do not try to break through the windshield. Use side and rear windows instead
2. Cover the patient and tell them before breaking tempered glass, cutting roof, etc.
3. Choose a door that will not endanger a victim to force. Use hand tools to bend sheet metal away.
4. Provide initial medical care.
5. Protect victims at all times.
6. Displace the seat
7. Remove the windshield
8. Remove the steering wheel
9. Displace the dashboard
10. Displace the roof - improves visibility and fresh air, large exit route for the victim, might improve fear.
11. Stabilize and package patient

Chapter 27
Assisting Special Rescue Teams

1. Which of the following is one of the two greatest hazards at a confined-space incident?
   A. Electrical shock
   B. Fall/crush injuries
   C. Oxygen deficiency
   D. Engulfment

Answer – C
Reference - FFS, p 851

2. Which control zone has the largest perimeter?
   A. Hot zone
   B. Rescue area
   C. Cold zone
   D. Support zone

Answer – C
Reference - FFS, p 954

3. What is the most common type of rescue situation encountered by fire fighters?
   A. Elevator rescue
   B. Structure fire
   C. Collapsed structure
   D. Motor vehicle crash

Answer – D
Reference - FFS, p 850

4. Who is the responsible party for a technical rescue incident that occurs at a worksite or industrial facility?
   A. The IC
   B. The property owner
   C. The foreperson or supervisor
   D. The business owner

Answer – A
Reference - FFS, p

5. What is the minimum distance to park from downed power lines?
   A. 50 ft (15m)
   B. 100 n (30m)
   C. A distance equal to half the span between utility poles
   D. A distance equal to the span between utility poles

Answer – D
Reference - FFS, p 846

6. What is the term for soil removed from an excavation?
   A. Spoils
   B. Tailings
   C. Fines
   D. Waste

Answer – A
Reference - FFS, p 854

7. Which factor commonly limits the use of helicopters for victim transport?
   A. The effect of rotor wash on ground conditions
   B. Weather conditions
   C. Medical conditions that are exacerbated by flight
   D. Expense

Answer – B
Reference - FFS, p 845

8. Which of the following is an awareness-level technical rescue skill?
   A. Install lockout/tagout/isolation devices
   B. Identify victim location and condition
   C. Recognize hazards
   D. Access victims to provide first aid to them

Answer – C
Reference - FFS, p 850

Chapter 27

9. Which factor will have the greatest impact on how a technical rescue incident is conducted?
   A. Whether the victim is conscious
   B. Whether the victims are trapped or just unable to move
   C. Total reflex time for the required resources
   D. Whether the incident is a rescue or a body recovery

Answer – D
Reference - FFS, p

10. In a trench rescue, which step comes first?
    A. Shore up the collapse site
    B. Place a rescuer near the victim
    C. Assist the victim with a pole or rope
    D. Provide an air supply to the victim

Answer – A
Reference - FFS, p 853

11. How does exposure to liquefied petroleum gas affect the body?
    A. There is no effect; the gas is inert and nontoxic
    B. The gas displaces breathing air
    C. The gas is a neurological toxin
    D. The gas causes pulmonary edema

Answer – B
Reference – Occupational Medicine, p 558-9

12. What is the most common method of demarcating the control zones for an emergency incident site?
    A. Traffic cones
    B. Barrier tape
    C. Ropes
    D. Traffic barricades

Answer – B
Reference - FFS, p 954

Assisting Special Rescue Teams

13. What should be a basic point of emphasis when training with other departments for technical rescue incidents?
    A. SOPs
    B. Equipment inventory
    C. Terminology
    D. Organization

Answer – A
Reference - FFS, p

14. Which resource do utility companies have readily accessible that is often needed on technical rescue incidents?
    A. Heavy equipment
    B. Surveying equipment
    C. Field-portable office facilities
    D. Confined-space permits

Answer – A
Reference - FFS, p

15. Which of the following is one of the five guidelines that fire fighters should keep in mind when assisting rescue team members?
    A. Get the big picture
    B. Question the plan
    C. Act decisively
    D. Follow orders

Answer – D
Reference - FFS, p 841

16. What is a common cause of secondary collapse at a trench rescue incident?
    A. Shifting of debris
    B. Personnel at the edge of the trench
    C. Wall shear
    D. Terracing

Answer – B
Reference - FFS, p 854

17. Which method should rescuers use to detect the presence of a dangerous atmosphere?
    A. NFPA/DOT labels and placards
    B. Environmental indicators
    C. Sensory indicators
    D. Atmospheric monitoring

Answer – D
Reference - FFS, p 844

18. Which of the following is a correct action to take at a trench cave-in rescue?
    A. Approach from the wide end of the trench
    B. Remove spoils from the trench lip
    C. Keep personnel back from the cave-in site
    D. Begin shoring and stabilizing as soon as the victim's air supply has been established

Answer – C
Reference – FFS, p 854

19. What is the term for the area in which rescue operations are conducted?
    A. Entry zone
    B. Hot zone
    C. Warm zone
    D. Rescue area

Answer – B
Reference - FFS, p

20. What is the most commonly used color of barrier tape for marking the cold zone?
    A. Red
    B. Green
    C. Orange
    D. Yellow

Answer – D
Reference - FFS, p 843

21. In which types of incidents should an accountability system be established?
    A. Those requiring entry into IDLH atmosphere
    B. All incidents
    C. Incidents with victims
    D. Incidents involving more than a single company

Answer – B
Reference - FFS, p

22. What is the role of awareness-level rescuers in the assessment of a technical rescue situation?
    A. Overall size-up and determination of initial actions
    B. Continuous reassessment of the scene
    C. Evaluation of the incident action plan
    D. This is not an awareness-level responsibility

Answer – D
Reference - FFS, p

23. What does the "I" stand for in the FAILURE acronym?
    A. Improper technique attempted
    B. Inadequate rescue skills
    C. IC not in control
    D. Integrity not maintained

Answer – B. Failure to understand the environment, Additional medical problems not considered, Inadequate rescue skills. Lack of teamwork or experience, Underestimating the logistics of the incident, Rescue vs. recovery mode not considered, Equipment not mastered.
Reference - FFS, p 842

24. When should emergency medical care be started for trapped victims in a technical rescue incident?
    A. As soon as they are safely accessible
    B. After they are packaged
    C. Upon exiting the hazard zone
    D. Upon arrival at the medical group

Answer – A
Reference - FFS, p 844

Chapter 27

25. In a technical rescue incident, what is the next step after stabilization has taken place?
   A. Access
   B. Size-up
   C. Security
   D. Ventilation

Answer – A
Reference - FFS, p 844

26. Which of the following is the primary safety consideration in a building collapse?
   A. Cause of the collapse
   B. Number of victims
   C. Type of collapse
   D. Building stability

Answer – D
Reference - FFS, p 855

27. How does exposure to natural gas affect the body?
   A. There is no effect; natural gas is inert and nontoxic
   B. Natural gas causes swelling of the airways
   C. Natural gas interferes with cellular metabolism
   D. Natural gas acts as an asphyxiant

Answer – D
Reference – Occupational Medicine p 558-9

28. On a technical rescue incident, the first arriving _____ assumes command.
   A. Operations-level rescuer
   B. Company officer
   C. Responder with technical rescue training
   D. Chief officer

Answer – B
Reference - FFS, p 842, 848

29. In which control zone is decontamination performed?
    A. Warm zone
    B. Decontamination zone
    C. Support zone
    D. Cold zone

Answer – A
Reference - FFS, p 954

30. What is the function of lockout/tagout systems?
    A. Prevent unauthorized activation of machinery or electricity
    B. Deny entry to the public and the media
    C. Enforce accountability for rescuers entering the hazard zone
    D. Prevent theft or unauthorized use of apparatus and equipment

Answer – A
Reference - FFS, p 843, 1142

31. What is the term for preparing a victim for movement as a unit, often by using a long spine board or similar device?
    A. Evaluating
    B. Demobilizing
    C. Restraining
    D. Packaging

Answer – D
Reference - FFS, p

32. Which color of barrier tape is used to demarcate the hot zone at a technical rescue incident?
    A. Red
    B. Yellow
    C. White and red
    D. Black and yellow

Answer – A
Reference - FFS, p 843

33. What is used to stabilize the sides of an excavation?
   A. Bracing
   B. Sheeting
   C. Shoring
   D. Cribbing

Answer – C
Reference - FFS, p 1149

34. What is a fire fighter's initial objective during a confined-space incident?
   A. Stabilize the situation
   B. Secure the scene
   C. Make contact with the victim
   D. Call for needed resources

Answer – B
Reference - FFS, p 851

35. Which of the following is a valid principle for disentangling a victim from a wrecked automobile?
   A. There are no circumstances that justify taking shortcuts in patient stabilization
   B. Stabilize the patient before stabilizing the vehicle
   C. Treatment before transport
   D. Remove the vehicle from around the victim, not the victim through the wreckage

Answer – D
Reference - FFS, p 844

36. When does size-up begin?
   A. While the company is in transit to the call
   B. When the victim is located
   C. When the company is dispatched
   D. Once the facts are known

Answer – A
Reference - FFS, p

37. What is the step in the technical rescue incident process that follows removal of a victim?
   A. Security
   B. Treatment
   C. Transport
   D. Packaging

Answer – C
Reference - FFS, p 842

38. What is the only circumstance in which a victim should be moved prior to completion of initial care, assessment, stabilization, and treatment?
   A. The victim's life is in immediate danger
   B. The victim states he or she has no injuries
   C. The victim is hostile or uncooperative
   D. The victim's injuries are minor

Answer – A
Reference - FFS, p 845

39. Which of the following is a hazardous materials operations-level skill?
   A. Analyze the magnitude of an incident
   B. Conduct atmospheric monitoring
   C. Perform victim rescue and recovery
   D. Take product control measures

Answer – C
Reference - FFS, p 871

40. What is the area that surrounds the incident site and whose size is proportional to the hazards that exist?
   A. Control zone
   B. Hot zone
   C. Rescue area
   D. Red zone

Answer – B
Reference - FFS, p 954

Chapter 27

41. One task the firefighter will be called upon to perform at specialized incidents is to:
    A. Perform rigging for elevated victim rescue
    B. Establish barriers
    C. Wear encapsulating suits
    D. Perform specialized technical rescue

Answer – B
Reference - FFS, p 847

49. An area or space that is not designed for continuous occupancy and has limited openings for entering and exiting is known as a:
    A. Confined space
    B. Collapse zone
    C. Watertight vessel
    D. Trench environment

Answer – B
Reference - FFS, p 847

Notes on Assisting Special Rescue Teams

Number of fires and loss from fires have decreased, so fire departments have taken on additional roles
  1. EMS
  2. HAZMAT - 55 gallons of material for technical HAZMAT call
  3. Technical rescue - underwater, swift water, high angle, trench and confined space, vehicle and machinery extrication, structural collapse, wilderness
  4. Training - all have three levels, awareness, operations (defensive), and technician (operations).

Stages of Special Rescue
  1. Preparation - most specialist teams carry harnesses, small and light helmets, and jumpsuits, which are easier to move in.
  2. Response
  3. Arrival and size up
  4. Stabilization
  5. Access
  6. Disentanglement
  7. Removal
  8. Transport
  9. Scene security

Assisting Special Rescue Teams

10. Post-incident analysis

Standard things that awareness level personnel can do to assist
1. Size up and request for additional resources if needed
2. Ensure scene security
3. Address utility hazards
4. Obtain information from witnesses
5. Control bystanders
6. Extinguish fires
7. Assist with equipment
8. Provide patient care for victims or responders

Confined Spaces
1. Operations - must have a straight line of sight and a rope to hook in to.
2. Sample atmosphere and set up ventilation fan if necessary

Trench and Excavation Collapse
1. Often occurs when children play around a pile of sand which then collapses.
2. Victims cannot be pulled out but must be dug out instead.
3. Shoring will be done by technical rescue personnel.
4. Vibration or additional weight will likely result in secondary collapse.
5. Do not walk close to the edge of a collapsed area until the area has been stabilized.
6. If you must approach a trench, do so from the narrow end, where the soil is more stable.
7. Soil that is removed from an excavation is called a spoil pile.

Rope Rescue
1. Operations (low angle), technician (high angle)
2. Low angle - walkable terrain (such as an embankment) without needing to put all one's weight on the rope, typically less than 45 degrees. The rope is the secondary means of support. Often used when available footing is not adequate.
3. High angle - non-walkable terrain requiring all or most of one's weight on the rope, typically greater than 45 degrees. The rope is the primary means of support.
4. Do not step on ropes. Friction from shoes and boots, and cutting from glass and metal shards, quickly damages ropes.
5. Assistants may need to set up ropes and anchor points.

Structural Collapse
1. Expect to do a lot of digging, hauling, and other hard manual labor
2. Experts are trained in shoring techniques to prevent further collapse and protect and evacuate victims

Chapter 27

Water and Ice Rescue
1. Keep victims in sight
2. Deploy water rescue throw bags
3. Most common scenario is when a vehicle tries to drive through a pool of water and gets trapped. If the water is deep enough, the vehicle can be swept away.

Wilderness Search and Rescue
1. Can be outdoor enthusiasts who get lost, injured, or are unprepared. Also common are impaired patients (alcohol, drugs, dementia) who get lost.
2. It takes a lot of searchers to search for and find a lost person.

HAZMAT incidents
1. Operational level responsibilities - analyze the magnitude of the incident, plan an initial response, implement the planned response, evaluate the progress of the plan.

Elevator and Escalator Rescue
1. Elevator - Always cut power to a malfunctioning elevator and secure the power supply with lockout and tagout procedures.
2. Escalator - Stop escalator

Post-incident - complete report

Chapters 28 through 34
Cover HAZMAT and are not included in this study guide.

Chapter 35
covers Terrorism Awareness and is not included in this study guide

Chapter 36
Fire Prevention and Public Education

1. Which public fire safety education programs would be used for a group of children from pre-school through elementary school age?
   A. Change you Clock-Change your Battery
   B. Stop, Drop, and Roll
   C. Home inspections
   D. Fire safety for babysitters

Answer – B
Reference - FFS, p 1016

Chapter 37
Fire Detection, Protection, and Suppression Systems

1. Visible products of combustion are best detected by a(n) _____ detector.

   A. Ionization
   B. Photoelectric
   C. Infrared
   D. Ultraviolet

Answer – B
Reference - FFS, p 1036

2. Which extinguishing agent is generally used in total flooding or specialized systems?
   A. Pressurized air
   B. Powder
   C. Purple K
   D. Carbon dioxide

Answer – D
Reference - FFS, p 1064

3. Dry pipe systems are used:
   A. Where rapid activation is required
   B. In areas where water supply is limited
   C. In buildings that store valuable items
   D. In applications where freezing temperatures occur

Answer – D
Reference - FFS, p 1056

4. The full name of an OS&Y valve is the _____ valve.
   A. Outside stem and yoke
   B. Outside shield and yoke
   C. Outside, shut, and yoke
   D. Open stem and yoke

Answer – A
Reference - FFS, p 1051

5. A post indicator valve (PIV) is:
   A. Designed to control the head pressure at the outlet of a standpipe system
   B. A device to speed the operation of the dry pipe valve by detecting the decrease in air pressure
   C. A control valve that is mounted on a wall
   D. A control valve that is mounted on a vertical case

Answer – A
Reference - FFS, p 1051

6. When shutting down a wet-pipe sprinkler system, one should first turn off the main water control valve and:
   A. Close all riser indicating valves
   B. Disable the alarm check valve
   C. Open the exhauster to drain the system
   D. Drain the system

Answer – D
Reference - FFS, p 1058

Notes on Fire Detection, Protection, and Suppression Systems

Modern commercial buildings are required to have such systems.

Fire alarms
   1. False - Error in the system, Dust (sheetrock, sawdust) Detectors too close to the kitchen, malicious, nuisance (improper functioning of system), unwanted (non-emergency condition)
   2. Alerts occupants visually and audibly
   3. May alert the fire department, override doors and elevators
   4. May automatically activate fire suppression systems
   5. Components - initiation, notification, control panel (need to know where this is on preincident survey)
   6. Control panel - manages power supply, manages proper operation of the system, indicate source of alarm, may interface with other systems, silences alarm and resets system, may have a remote annunciator.
   7. Residential - single detector
   8. Types - ionization (invisible products of combustion) and photoelectric (visible products of combustion)
   9. Initiation - Manual (pull station, double action pull station), automatic (heat detectors including rate of rise and line, flame detectors, gas detectors such as carbon monoxide,

multiple gas), fire suppression systems (ensure that someone is aware that water is flowing)
10. Zoned and coded systems - locate alarm in building

Alarm notification
1. Local alarm system - notifies occupants but no one else, must still call 9112
2. Remote station system - fire department, 911 center3
3. Auxiliary - building system tied into master alarm system
4. Proprietary - connected directly to monitoring site owned by building owner
5. Central station - third party, off site

Suppression

Sprinkler - fire detection and suppression, components (head, piping, control valve, water supply).
1. Head - body, release mechanism, detector spraying pattern, fusible link metal alloy melts to allow water flow when specified temperature is reached. Frangible bulk sprinkler head, chemical pellet sprinkler head, special sprinkler head, deluge heads (no cap to release water)
2. Temperature ratings (165 degrees in light hazard occupancy)
3. Mounting for up, down, or sideways spray
4. Piping
5. Valves - main water supply control (shut sprinkler down to reset), alarm valve, other
6. Water supply - municipal water supply, on-site storage tank, or static water sources
7. Fire pumps - used when water comes from a static source, can boost pressure
8. Fire Department Connection - allow engine to pump water into a sprinkler system
9. Water flow alarm - monitors water flow through system
10. Types - wet (water constantly in the system, held back), dry (pressurized air keeps valve down and holds water back), preaction (secondary device must activate before water flows if air pressure is lost), deluge
11. Residential sprinkler systems reduce fire deaths by 82%

Standpipe -
1. Class 1 - 2 ½ inch male coupling and valve to open the water supply
2. Network of pipes and outlets for fire hoses
3. On each floor of a multifloor building
4. Class 2 - 1 ½ inch single jacket hose preconnect to allow occupants to attack the fire.
5. Class 3 - combination of class 1 and class two systems
6. Flow restriction and pressure reducing devices
7. Wet standpipe - use municipal water
8. Dry standpipe

Chapter 37

Specialized extinguishing systems
1. Where water would not be useful to extinguish a fire
2. Commercial kitchen
3. Electrical
4. Other

Chapter 38
Fire Cause Determination

1. Which would be a type or form of evidence that could be found at a fire scene?
   A. Water damage
   B. Trailers
   C. Properly stored containers of ignitable liquids
   D. Overhaul damage

Answer – B
Reference - FFS, p 1082

2. Fire officials investigating a building fire may prevent owners and occupants from reentering until:
   A. They are cleared as suspects
   B. They can be accomplished by fire department personnel
   C. An insurance representative arrives
   D. They cleared by certified fire investigators

Answer – D
Reference - FFS, p 1084

3. Which is one of the normal observations that firefighters make to assist in determining fire cause?
   A. The number and location of observers
   B. Hindrances to firefighting
   C. People leaving the fire scene in a hurry
   D. How the fire reacted to water application

Answer – B
Reference - FFS, p 1082

4. Depth of char is:
   A. Related to the intensity of the fire at a particular location
   B. Always linked to the use of an accelerant in starting the fire
   C. Conclusive evidence of arson
   D. A reliable indicator of the fire's point of origin

Answer – A
Reference - FFS, p 1075

Chapter 38

Notes on Fire Investigation

Primary References
1. NFPA 921 and 1033
2. Fire Investigator - Principles and Practices
3. Kirk's Fire Investigation
4. Scientific Protocols for Fire Investigation - John Lentini
5. Investigator modules - CFItrainer.net

Basic Fire Methodology

Mindset of a Fire Investigator
1. Get out of the mental firefighter mode - take time to investigate the fire rather than the urgent action of fighting the fire.
2. Just because you cannot see it doesn't mean it is not happening
3. Evidence remaining at the scene is pivotal.

People interested in fire investigation
1. Those who want a career in fire investigation
2. Those firefighters who want to help their department
3. Those who were looking for something else to do

Scientific Method Applied to Fire Investigation
1. Identify the need to answer a question
2. Research Question - What caused this fire?
3. Initial evidence review
4. Generate hypothesis
5. Hypothesis - This fire was caused by (fuel spill, open flame, intentional, etc.)
6. Collect pertinent and comprehensive evidence - interviews, observations, laboratory support
7. Analyze evidence
8. Prove or disprove hypothesis - inductive reasoning, beware preconceptions
9. If proved, prepare to testify. Tell a story.
10. If disproved, generate new hypothesis and repeat process
11. Systematic approach - doing things the same way, the right way, and in the same order each time, tailored to the individual fire scene
12. Follow up investigation

Sources of information
1. Reporting - West Virginia fire marshal's hotline (formerly Arson Hotline)
2. Dispatch call (caller and dispatcher) and notes
3. Radio traffic during call
4. Initial 360° review
5. Observations - fire, law, EMS, victims, home occupant, owner, onlookers
6. Physical data - gas cans, flammable fluid or gas tanks, flame sources, fire accelerants
7. Victim - burns on bodies of victims, other characteristics
8. Fire scene photographs, including drones
9. Experimental support - test burn of a similar article
10. Lab support - samples (carpet with irregular burn pattern, etc.)

Determining the Origin of a Fire
1. Examine the scene and exterior of the building
2. The area of the heaviest damage (including the greatest depth of char) is usually the area of origin of the fire
3. 95% of fires begin as compartment fires
4. Products of combustion naturally go up and out ("V pattern"). Look for the V pattern on the wall next to the fire
5. Point of origin is usually at the base of the V.
6. Different burn patterns suggest unnatural activity. For example, an inverted V could occur because flammable fuel was poured on the wall. More likely, it could also occur because of limited ventilation; the fire below was moving towards a source of limited air above.

Four components of investigation
1. Heat - what was the ignition source?
2. Fuel - what was ignited first?
3. Oxygen - usually ambient air
4. Event (chemical chain reaction) - what happened in the actual event being investigated?
5. The fire will die if at least one of these four components are eliminated.

Legal Considerations

How can your property be entered, and searched if needed?
1. Your written (or recorded verbal) permission. You need consent from all of the legal occupants of the building (marital property - one required, independent occupants - consent from each occupant). Ask prosecutor if unsure, but if in doubt, get consent from every adult. Consent lasts for 24-48 hours and can be revoked at any time.

2. Public investigation - Search warrants - Issued by magistrates and circuit court judges on probable cause that a crime was committed. Search warrants apply to law enforcement duties only. Best to photograph building from public space to get search warrant.
3. Private investigation - may require consent from property owner
4. Common practice based on exigent circumstance - Fire departments have control of a fire scene for 24 to 48 hours after a fire. Get the investigation done in that time frame. However, this may not be reliable.
5. Entering a scene without authority may result in criminal charges (trespassing, theft if anything is removed), an action for civil liability (destruction of property if excessive damage is done), and/or inadmissible evidence at trial (fruit of toxic tree).
6. Firefighters must consider security of scene and preservation of fire patterns and potential evidence.
7. Fire scene investigation is a search and seizure.
8. Administrative search warrants - not available in West Virginia but available in other states.
9. The simple presence of a fire does not by itself constitute "probable cause."

Investigations
1. All aspects can be scrutinized
2. Legal proceedings may be criminal or civil
3. Laws change within a jurisdiction or vary by jurisdiction.
4. Investigator can testify as an expert witness, and must be familiar with applicable laws
5. Authority to conduct the investigation - law (public sector), contract (private sector investigations)
6. Arson immunity reporting acts - there is an exchange of information between public officials and insurance companies. These also require insurance companies to report criminal fires
7. Licensing - may be licensed as a private investigator.

Private sector investigator
1. No constitutional issues
2. Consent - express consent from owner or legal occupant (squatters not included) or implied consent from insurance policy. Courts can grant a right of entry.

Witness Interviews and Interrogation
1. Fifth Amendment - person cannot be compelled to give incriminating testimony.
2. Sixth Amendment - person has a right to counsel. If a person is in a "custodial" setting, meaning that the person does not feel like they have the right or ability to leave, they must be offered the right to counsel (Miranda advisement). If the person is in a "non-custodial" setting, Miranda is not required. Different jurisdictions have different standards. "Custodial settings" include arrest and detention.

3. Record every interview that you do, get the interviewees permission to record the interview, and advise them that they have the right to leave at any time.
4. Interviews are an exchange of information
5. Custodial setting factors - authority of the interview, location of the interview, length and context of the interview, participants at the interview.

Spoliation of Evidence
1. Loss, destruction, or alteration of evidence by the person responsible for it.
2. When an investigator moves or removes material, other parties cannot investigate it.
3. Parties responsible can be charged with tampering with evidence or face civil penalties.
4. Insurance companies look to recoup the money that they paid out. They can sue companies or fire departments to recoup.
5. In one case, the incident commander at the fire scene took a space heater from a fire scene to train his members on electrical fires. After training, he threw the space heater into the dumpster. The trash company took it away.
6. Avoid claims - alert parties of interest to evidence in their interest. Secure the scene (at least fire tape). Document the scene. Do not needlessly discard, destroy, or lose evidence. Scene documentation software is available.

Reports
1. Report content - procedural rules, usual practice, and attorney requirements.
2. Accurate, detailed, and easy to read.
3. Types of evidence - real (physical), demonstrative (demonstrating a principle that you think occurred at a fire scene), documentary (videos, audio, field notes), and testimonial
4. Field notes - Consider destroying field notes after submitting the report. Field notes are preliminary and may not communicate conclusions clearly. These notes are discoverable by the courts. However, destroy all field notes, not just a few.

Systems to give a 360-degree view of a fire scene
1. Originally developed for realtors
2. Matterport system
3. Provides every measurement from inside rooms
4. Layered, so can show evidence including still photos of specific scene and text

Fire Investigator Requirements
1. NFPA 921 - Used as standard of care for Investigation of Fires and Explosions. No language such as "shall" or "must" because the authors intend this to be a guide. If you do not use 921, you need to be able to explain why you didn't.
2. On-seen personnel - fire investigators, fire analysts, technicians who analyze evidence, other experts with specialized areas of expertise.

Chapter 38

3. NFPA 1033 - Nationally applicable minimum job performance requirements for fire investigators. They must be evaluated. The National Association of Fire Investigators offered certifications for fire, explosion, vehicle, and other investigators.
4. Firefighters are expected to determine origin and cause for fires that they work. However, they do not have to meet these standards.

Fire Science
1. Fire is a chemical reaction (oxidation). It only occurs when materials are in the gas phase. Heated solids produce liquids which go to gas or produce gases directly by pyrolysis. Heated liquids vaporize directly to the gas phase.
2. Fuel sources - organic (carbon containing) is most common and liquids are most dangerous
3. Phase changes can be reversible (melting, vaporization) or irreversible (thermal decomposition). Charring of wood is an example of the later.
4. Flame types - Premixed (natural gas with air), and Diffusion (candle flame)
5. Products of combustion - smoke (soot, ash, liquid droplets, and fire gases). These products migrate away (up and out) from the fire and cool, accumulating on horizontal and vertical surfaces. If heated, they will ignite.
6. Do not rely on smoke or flame color as an indicator of what is burning. Color can be changed by phase for materials, and by ventilation and other firefighter operations.
7. Ceiling jet - movement of gases parallel to the ceiling

Heat transfer
1. Heat energy transfers from areas of higher to lower temperature. Heat flux (rate of heat transfer in kilowatts per square meter)
2. Temperature - measurement of molecular activity when compared to a reference or standard
3. Heat - amount of energy needed to change an object's temperature, Transferred by conduction, convection, or radiation.
4. Heat transfers in a wave pattern similar to the sea water going in and out on the seashore.

Thermometry
1. Empirical scales based on the activity of water, including boiling and freezing (F/C)
2. Thermodynamic scales based on absolute zero (Kelvin, Rankine)

Fuel
1. Fuel load - Amount of fuel present
2. Fuel items - materials consumed during a fire
3. Fuel package - fuel items placed close enough together so that flames can spread.

Heat release rate

Fire Cause Determination

1. Heat release rate - how fast heat is being released (free burning to flashover to smoldering and decay), bell curve shape
2. Larger flame heights have higher rates of heat release

Compartment fire spread
1. Fuel controlled - controlled by amount of fuel in the room.
2. Vent controlled - controlled by amount of ventilation in the room. As fire destroys the room, airflow into the room may increase, promoting ventilation.

Fire Effects and Fire Patterns
1. Effects
2. Patterns - V shape
3. Physical evidence - burned materials and by products
4. Pattern interpretation changes over time.
5. Melting and distortion can help determine the melting temperatures of common materials.
6. Mass loss - can help determine duration and intensity of a fire. Can also help identify where fire started and developed.
7. Char - carbonaceous material resulting from burning
8. Spalling - chipping or pitting of concrete or masonry on floors, walls, and ceilings. It may show different coloration, may be caused by heat or mechanical stress, and may have existed prior to the fire.

Communicator Questions
1. Exact address of the caller and the incident
2. What exactly is the caller seeing?
3. Anyone injured, deceased, or trapped in the fire?
4. Are there usual occupants in this structure?
5. Are there exposures around the fire scene which are in danger?
6. Did the caller see how the fire started?
7. Did the caller see anyone running to or from the scene?
8. Any vehicles drive to or from the scene?
9. Any unusual sounds prior to the discovery of the fire (gunshot, explosion, glass breaking, other unusual sounds)?
10. Any unusual activity in the area recently or prior to the fire?
11. Call duration?
12. Make sure that each caller for a specific fire is interviewed completely, as each one will have different information.

Get bystander videos when possible.

Chapter 38

Oxidation
1. Non-Combustible materials - color and texture changes, and changes in fire patterns
2. Worse oxidation occurs with higher temperature and longer exposure

A fire scene is nothing more than a collection of indicators of how and where heat moved.

Smoke deposits
1. Soot may collect on cooler surfaces such as walls and windows
2. Color and texture do not indicate burning or heat release rate
3. Sonic staining - nature of soot detection on smoke alarms can show whether the smoke alarm sounded during a fire. Staining will occur the speaker of a smoke alarm.
4. "Clean burn" - As fire grows, it consumes smoke deposits from earlier in the fire. This may indicate the area of origin.
5. Direct flame contact or radiant heat exposure produces clean areas on noncombustible surfaces bordered by dark areas.

Calcination
1. Plaster or gypsum surfaces (drywall)
2. Chemically bound water is released by heat
3. Reacts predictably - paper burns off, then color changes
4. Rate and depth do not indicate burn times. They are affected by breaching (holes in drywall, characteristics of fire.

Glass effects
1. Deposits of soot usually indicate early failure of the glass before accumulation of smoke.
2. May result from rapid heating, damage prior to fire, and direct flame impingement
3. Finding unsooted glass at a fire scene suggests that the glass was not there when the fire began.
4. The glass in incandescent light bulbs will melt and bubble in the direction that the heat was traveling.
5. Fractured glass is found in most structure fires. Windowpanes may pop out of frames. Crazing results of rapid cooling of glass rather than from heating

Furniture springs
1. Annealing - metal has lost its temper and it begins to sag. This provides clues on fire intensity, duration, and direction of travel.
2. Does not indicate type of fire.

Heat shadowing

Fire Cause Determination

1. Caused by an object blocking travel of heat to a surface - radiated heat, convected heat, and direct flame.
2. Creates a discontinuous pattern
3. When a person is standing in front of a wall during an explosion and the person is killed but the wall behind shows a silhouette of the person.
4. Protected areas - object is shielded from heat transfer, combustion, and deposition. They are useful in reconstructing a fire scene.

Rainbow effect
1. Oil and water do not mix. Oil floats on the water's surface, and that interference pattern produces a "rainbow" effect.
2. Produced by asphalt, plastic, and wood products
3. Asphalt - burned asphalt shoveled back into burnt car contaminates car with petroleum products

Fire patterns
1. Analyze fire patterns
2. Used to determine sequence of events
3. Patterns at origin may be destroyed if fire grows

Plume-generated patterns
1. Circular on ceiling but V shaped on walls
2. Inverted cone patterns - vent flow (fire seeks ventilation above)
3. Hourglass shape
4. U shaped - larger fires
5. Pointer and arrow
6. As plume develops, size and shape of pattern changes

Ventilation-generated patterns
1. As pressure builds during combustion, hot gases, and fire escape through openings with increased velocity. Damage increases because heat is transferred to sides of the vent point by conduction in addition to radiation.
2. Well-ventilated fire increases the rate of material damage.
3. Heavy damage is found at ventilation points, even if they are not the point of origin.

Hot gas layer generated patterns
1. Prior to flashover, the hot gas layer begins to descend (banking down).
2. Line of descent can be determined by examining the line of demarcation.
3. Can be called a containment pattern.
4. Whole room affected - Lines of demarcation can be found on all surfaces. Original fire patterns gone.

Chapter 38

Patterns detected in fire victim's injuries
1. Do not move body until it has been documented and analyzed
2. Heat effects - Skin will redden, darken, blister, splits, and char, Muscle will dehydrate, contract, and shrink, "Pugilistic pose"
3. Treat bodies as evidence

Pattern location
1. Drone footage - large scale roof patterns
2. Wiring insulation - small scale patterns
3. Created as heat moves across surfaces

Beveling
1. Indicator of direction of fire on wood wall studs
2. Bevel leans in direction of fire travel
3. Radiant heat, isolated smoldering objects, and ventilation.
4. Downward movement is not necessarily from an ignitable liquid. Ventilation is a major cause, because gas may have been forced through small holes in the flooring.
5. Direction of fire travel is determined by patterns
6. If a flammable liquid is suspected, submit samples for laboratory analysis.

Taking samples from fire scenes - Consider chain of custody

Pattern Analysis
1. Heat pattern – usually V shaped from the ignition point and up

Cause of fire
1. Accidental - stove on, food cooking, extension cords
2. Natural - lightning,
3. Incendiary - set fire
4. Undetermined - cannot tell what happened

Expert witnesses can give opinion-based testimony

Quadranting
1. Break structure or area into four specific parts for evaluation
2. Label corners AB, BC, CD, and DA IAW normal fire terminology.

Fire Cause Determination
1. Investigators must identify - ignition source, first fuel ignited, oxidizing agent, and potential human actions. Consider other factors involved.

2. Ignition source - provide sufficient energy and can transfer the energy to the first fuel long enough to bring it to ignition temperature. Arcing 110 Amp current electrical energy in a house can ignite paper. This includes generation, transmission, and heating.
3. First fuel ignited - surface to mass ratio inversely proportional to energy required to ignite. Wood shavings ignite faster than a wooden block.
4. Oxidizing agent - fire intensity can be enhanced by other oxidants such as medical oxygen. Look for unusual oxidants.
5. Ignition sequence - must determine how it all fit together. Evaluate all potential sources. Testing alternative hypotheses will rule in or out possibilities. Look for diffuse fuel ignitions, multiple origins, trailers, witnessed ignitions, presence of ignitable liquids.

Put the ignition story together
1. How did the first fuel get to be present?
2. How did the ignition source get to be present?
3. How did the oxidizers get to be present?
4. How did the subsequent heat move through the area?

Made in the USA
Thornton, CO
11/07/24 14:38:27

a231184a-ae6d-4e08-bf5c-15dee508e9f8R01